Dear Reader:

The book you are about to read is the latest bestseller from the St. Martin's True Crime Library, the imprint *The New York Times* calls "the leader in true crime!" The True Crime Library offers you fascinating accounts of the latest, most sensational crimes that have captured the national attention. St. Martin's is the publisher of John Glatt's riveting and horrifying SECRETS IN THE CELLAR, which shines a light on the man who shocked the world when it was revealed that he had kept his daughter locked in his hidden basement for 24 years. In the Edgar-nominated WRITTEN IN BLOOD, Diane Fanning looks at Michael Petersen, a Marine-turned-novelist found guilty of beating his wife to death and pushing her down the stairs of their home—only to reveal another similar death from his past. In the book you now hold, DEATH ON THE RIVER, Diane Fanning returns to examine a deadly episode on the Hudson River.

St. Martin's True Crime Library gives you the stories behind the headlines. Our authors take you right to the scene of the crime and into the minds of the most notorious murderers to show you what really makes them tick. St. Martin's True Crime Library paperbacks are better than the most terrifying thriller, because it's all true! The next time you want a crackling good read, make sure it's got the St. Martin's True Crime Library logo on the spine—you'll be up all night!

Charles E. Spicer, Jr.
Executive Editor, St. Martin's True Crime Library

ALSO BY DIANE FANNING

Available in print and e-book format from the
True Crime Library of St. Martin's Paperbacks

DEATH
ON THE
RIVER

DIANE FANNING

St. Martin's Paperbacks

DEATH ON THE RIVER

Copyright © 2019 by Diane Fanning.

All rights reserved.

For information address St. Martin's Press, 175 Fifth Avenue, New York, NY 10010.

ISBN: 978-1-250-09204-5

Our books may be purchased in bulk for promotional, educational, or business use. Please contact your local bookseller or the Macmillan Corporate and Premium Sales Department at 1-800-221-7945, ext. 5442, or by e-mail at MacmillanSpecialMarkets@macmillan.com.

Printed in the United States of America

St. Martin's Paperbacks edition / May 2019

St. Martin's Paperbacks are published by St. Martin's Press, 175 Fifth Avenue, New York, NY 10010.

10 9 8 7 6 5 4 3 2 1

TO VINCENT ALEXANDER VIAFORE
AND THE FRIENDS AND FAMILY
WHO KEEP HIS MEMORY ALIVE

DEATH
ON THE
RIVER

CHAPTER ONE

A brilliant sun warmed the air on a mid-April Sunday afternoon—a day that shouted with joy that spring had arrived at last. The lovely weather drew many New Yorkers outdoors to revel in the departure of the cold and gloomy winter. Among them were 46-year-old Vincent Viafore and his fiancée, 35-year-old Angelika Graswald.

Vincent was an attractive man with dark hair that was beginning to recede. His brown downturned eyes appeared mournful, but for the perpetual twinkle residing in their depths. His crooked, puckish grin readily expanded into a room-brightening smile. His physique made it obvious that he'd remained physically active into his forties.

The high cheekbones and deep-set eyes in Angelika's heart-shaped face hinted at her Russian ethnicity. Her petite stature and perky, flirtatious demeanor added an elfin quality to her appearance.

The couple set out from their home in Poughkeepsie, New York, on the east side of the Hudson, with a pair of kayaks—Vince's blue one strapped to the roof of his white Jeep Cherokee and Angelika's red one stowed inside.

Before leaving town, they made two stops on Main Street: one at Wendy's for a bite to eat and another at the Sunoco service station where Angelika bought cigarettes.

They traversed the river to the west side on the Franklin D. Roosevelt Mid-Hudson Bridge, decorated with portraits of Franklin and Eleanor. The Ulster County side of the river greeted them with an awe-inspiring, fortress-like wall of chiseled gray stone rising on their left. They drove less than twenty miles down 9W, a busy, winding two-lane highway scattered with towns and villages, meandering through seedy stretches, stunning locales, and historic markers.

They turned left at the entrance of the Kowawese Unique Area and New Windsor's Plum Point Park, more than one hundred acres of idyllic natural land with striking views of the river and mountains. A short drive took them away from the hustle and bustle and into the shade of black walnut trees, white oaks, and cottonwoods. The small paved road soon turned to dirt and opened up on to a small sandy beach, with picnic tables by the rockier section of coast, and hiking trails—a favorite spot for fishermen, peace seekers, and people launching canoes and kayaks out onto the Hudson.

The 315-mile waterway, named for explorer Henry Hudson, is the largest river wholly contained in the boundaries of New York State. The Hudson originates in Lake Tear of the Clouds on the southwest slope of Mount Marcy, the highest mountain in the Adirondacks. It flows through the Hudson Valley and into the Atlantic Ocean in New York City, where it forms the geographical boundary between New York and New Jersey.

Looking from the park, where Angelika and Vince launched their kayaks, across the river, the most prominent sight is the stony outcrop of Pollepel Island, named for a local legend about an ethereal young girl named Polly Pell who was once stranded there. More often referred to as Bannerman Island, named after its original developer, the spit of land snuggled close to the eastern bank, at a point where the river was a formidable expanse, narrowing a little farther down into a faster water chute.

With calm waters that afternoon, the vastness of the river didn't appear overwhelming to the active, athletic couple. Around 4:15, Vince and Angelika climbed into their vessels and set off across the river for their mile-and-a-quarter journey. Stupendous views of the Hudson Highlands' delightfully named Storm King Mountain, Breakneck Ridge, and Bull Hill served as a backdrop and added to the ambiance of their goal: the oft-romanticized six-and-a-half-acre island. The patch of land was dominated by stunning ruins resembling a falling Scottish castle, the remains of a building erected for a far more utilitarian purpose—as a storage facility.

The historical significance of this isle near West Point began during the Revolutionary War, when American forces ran a chain across the Hudson in a failed attempt to prevent the passage of British ships up the river. In the late nineteenth century, Francis Bannerman IV, a Scottish immigrant, collected weapons and ammunition from the Spanish-American War and the Civil War for resale. He stuffed it all into a storeroom in New York City but did not have the space to safely store the 30 million surplus munitions cartridges he had on hand. With that in mind, he purchased the island in 1901 and began construction of a home and an arsenal with a sign reading: "Bannerman's Island Arsenal" installed into the west-facing side of the building. Construction ceased in 1918 when Bannerman died. On August 15, 1920, the powder house exploded with enough force to shatter windows in nearby towns and send chunks of rock onto the railroad tracks onshore. New York State bought the property in 1967, cleared out the military merchandise, and conducted tours until an incredibly ferocious fire ripped through the grounds in 1969, causing massive damage to the buildings.

The structures were abandoned and neglected until 1995, when a Brooklyn Realtor, Neal Caplan, moved his business to the town of Beacon and began the process of restoring the island. The ruins, on the one hand, remained fragile and precarious, with propped-up walls. The crumbling castle-like warehouse was cracked, pocked with holes, and surrounded by rubble. The former arsenal was overgrown with vines and other vegetation and its upper floors appeared ready to cave in with the slightest misstep.

The gardens, on the other hand, were glorious. Francis Bannerman's wife, Helen, had created a cutting garden, a woodland landscaping, as well as elaborate herb and vegetable patches. Caplan founded the Bannerman Island Trust, an organization dedicated to preserving the historic island, and directed a true-to-the-period reconstruction of the gardens and its maintenance, with the help of volunteers such as Angelika.

Angelika had fallen in love at first sight with the quirky island, the romance of the ruins, and the very presence of a castle in New York. As a native of Europe, she was used to seeing castles all over the place, and finding one here was a surprise that embraced her heart like the comfort of home.

Before setting out from Plum Point a little before 5:00 that afternoon, Angelika sent a text to Barbara Gottlock, Bannerman's volunteer coordinator, who lived up on a hill within sight of the island. "Hi, Barb, we're kayaking today out of Plum Point and I'd like to stop on the island since I won't be able to make it there this Wednesday. Please let me know if it's a problem," she wrote. "Otherwise, I'll give you an update on how the geese are doing."

They waited a few minutes for a response and passed

the time chatting with a fisherman on the shore. As a volunteer, Angelika knew that she wasn't supposed to visit the historic site outside of scheduled gardening hours, unless she was in an official tour group.

Not willing to wait any longer to hear back from Barbara, she paddled off with Vince, crossing the water to the island with no difficulty. They landed at the harbor near the southeast corner of the island and mounted the steps that led to the residence. Over the next two hours, they engaged in physical intimacy as they rambled through the gardens and castle grounds. Angelika posed for provocative photographs in lingerie she'd packed for the trip, and Vince enjoyed the two beers he'd brought along.

Together they roamed the island, posing for pictures, checking out the status of the bulbs Angelika had planted the previous year, and simply enjoying the afternoon. During their relaxing stroll, the sky darkened with ominous clouds gathering above the river. A sharp gust caused the few brown never-say-die leaves clinging to branches to rattle like snakes. A clear warning that the weather was changing for the worse.

At one point, the couple climbed into their kayaks and attempted to navigate around the island to get to the beach area on the other side. The roughness of the water, however, made it impossible, so they returned to resume their photo session with Angelika's iPhone and Vince's camera.

Just before 7:00 pm, Wesley Gottlock, Bannerman's tour coordinator and Barbara's husband, pointed his telescope down to the island below. "I think there are trespassers on the island—a man and a woman," he told his wife.

"What are they doing?" Barbara asked.

"The woman looks like she's dancing around and posing for a guy who's taking photos," Wesley said. A few minutes later, he added, "They're down on the dock now."

Barbara checked her cell phone to see if anyone had messaged her about a visitor and saw the text from Angelika. She wasn't authorized to give permission to anyone to visit the island unattended and so didn't comment on that question. She just texted back: "I think we saw you out there on the dock? How were the geese?"

Angelika replied at 7:04: "We're leaving now. I'll send more pics later. Geese are here."

The sun was low on the horizon when Vince and Angelika set out to return to the mainland at 7:30 that evening. The wind had gained intensity and drove the air in the opposite direction of the tidal current, creating chop and instability. The nice, balmy day was now a memory as a chill filled the air, bringing the temperature closer to the frigid 46 degrees of the river itself.

As experienced as they were as kayakers, they were not familiar with this section of the Hudson, where the river approached the narrows and flowed with increased vigor even on a calm day. Surprisingly, they did not follow standard safety procedures. Typically, any kayaker would wear a personal flotation device (PFD) or life jacket at all times, whether traveling across a roiling sea or a placid pond. In New York, the law specifically required that precaution from November 1 to May 1 every year. Angelika wore a PFD, but Vince did not. In addition, neither wore a dry suit with a base layer for added protection—a habit most kayakers followed until mid-May, when the Hudson's water temperature finally reached sixty degrees.

To complicate matters further, their white-water vessels were not well suited for the conditions on this notorious river. Longer boats—like a thirteen- to fifteen-foot-long touring kayak with twin bulkheads—were recommended to ensure the required buoyancy in rough conditions.

At first, Vince enjoyed the challenge of the wild river

and played around in his kayak like an excited boy in his first inflatable raft. He pulled in front of Angelika's kayak and shouted, "Baby, this is an adventure of a lifetime!"

Exactly what happened after that lighthearted moment in the choppy water is up for debate, with conflicting conjectures and story lines. But one thing remains fatally clear—the perilous waves swamped Vince's kayak and he ended up in the brutal, cold water, separated from his kayak in conditions where his chances for survival were slim.

"I saw him struggling a bit," Angelika said later. "He was trying to paddle the waves because they were getting crazy and then I just saw him flip." Once Vince was in the frigid water, she said, "he kept watching me, and I kept watching him."

In flip-flops, shorts, and a T-shirt, Vince was defenseless against the intense cold. He grabbed for the kayak and tried to hold on tight. With every passing minute, his grip grew more tenuous, his movements clumsier, as his motor skills deteriorated and the symptoms of hypothermia began to set in. Soon he was hyperventilating, faster and deeper breaths with every passing second. Spontaneous shivering racked his body, his teeth chattered uncontrollably. His blood pressure would have dropped. His core body temperature would have plummeted. The cold would have felt like a physical presence, a heavy weight wrapped around his chest, pressing in, making him gasp for air, squeezing the life out of his body. Within ten minutes in that frigid temperature, his lungs would have collapsed. It is a cruel death, as desperation builds and panic overcomes cogent thought.

If Angelika was just looking on as he struggled, Vince endured more than physical torture, his emotions overcome with the horror of love betrayed for the last few moments of his life. Angelika, however, claimed that she tried to get to him, shouting, "Just hold on—just hold on!"

At one point, she reported that he said, "I don't think I'm going to make it."

But she minimized his fear: "Pfft, what are you talking about? You're going to make it, of course."

CHAPTER TWO

After Vince had spent twenty minutes in the water, Angelika called 911: "Hi, uh, I'm in the Hudson River. My fiancé fell in the water. Can you please call anybody?"

"Just tell me exactly what happened," the operator said.

"We were kayaking—my fiancé flipped over. He's in the water right now."

"Stay on the phone with me, okay? Does he have a life vest on?"

"He has something he's holding on to, but it's getting very bad. I can't get to him, it's very windy, and the waves are coming in— Oh my God! I'm in a red kayak, but he fell in. I couldn't swim to him. I couldn't paddle to him. He's getting further and further away from me! The waves are very strong. I can see his—still see his head. He's going to drown, please call somebody!"

For a moment, the 911 dispatcher and Angelika couldn't hear each other well. The operator could only hear distant cries as she repeated Angelika's name over and over.

Finally, Angelika's words grew clear again. "I don't see him anymore," she said with a choking sob.

"Okay, we've got help on the way. Okay? Did he have a life vest on when he flipped over?"

"He had a little floating thing, not a vest."

"He didn't have a vest, but he had something to help him float?"

"But I don't see him. Oh my God!"

"Can you see the kayak still?"

"No, the kayak went underwater. Oh my God."

A woman at the nearby Cornwall Yacht Club spotted Angelika in her kayak being buffeted about by the current. She called Jim Schaack, the club's Commodore. Three members climbed aboard the work boat and went to the rescue.

"We've got a boat in the water heading down to you, okay?"

"Okay. The water is very cold. I'm afraid he's— Oh my God. I think he's drowned. I just need him to be rescued."

"Can you make your way over to the Cornwall Yacht Club where you see the lights?"

"Yes."

"Start paddling toward that way, okay?"

"I'm not worried about myself, I'm worried about him."

"I understand. I understand."

"Okay. I'm going to push around a little bit."

"That's fine. Just keep the phone on."

"Yes. I see the club now."

"Where did you guys go into the river?"

"The boat is coming towards me right now."

"Good. Put the phone down, just keep it open for me, okay?"

"Okay. Okay."

Suddenly Angelika's kayak capsized. The dispatcher heard odd noises but couldn't decipher their meaning. She continued talking. "Where did you guys go in at?"

But she got no response. "Angelika?" she shouted.

* * *

On April 19, 2015, just before 8:00 pm, State Troopers Andrew Freeman and Jason Vidacovich overheard the Orange County dispatch sending the Village of Cornwall-on-Hudson Police Department to the Cornwall Yacht Club. They responded to the call to determine if state resources were needed at the river.

Local police officer Stephen Bedetti was not working a shift that evening, but he'd gone into the New Windsor police station to catch up on paperwork. When the call for help came in to the dispatcher, Bedetti agreed to respond to the kayakers overturning in the Hudson River. His usual police vehicle was being used by his regular partner, and his bag was in that car. He wished he had it, since it contained his notebook and other materials he liked to have on hand. Nonetheless, he reported to the landing near the Cornwall Yacht Club. He was met by a local fire department chief and a village police officer, who updated him on the situation. The three men walked over to the shoreline and the gazebo there. A local woman joined them to watch the unfolding drama.

They all looked out at the river in the direction of New Windsor to the spot where the kayakers were thought to have overturned. Bedetti saw an object that could have been a person in the water. The volunteer rescue boat sped over to that spot.

Down by the river, the search response was escalating with every passing moment. More boats left the yacht club and headed out to search. Flashing lights filled the air around Cornwall-on-Hudson and soon a helicopter with a searchlight was scanning the water.

Meanwhile, Officer Bedetti boarded the volunteer rescue boat as it returned to shore. The people on board had wrapped Angelika in blankets. She shivered uncontrollably when he asked her name.

"What happened? Where were you coming from?" he asked, walking off the boat with her toward the approaching paramedics. She carried a black bag and a life vest and told her rescuers that Vince was still in the water. As soon as she disembarked, the club members turned the boat around and went back upriver to search for him, joining the ever-growing number of law enforcement boats taking to the water.

Angelika turned to Bedetti. "We were coming from Bannerman's Island on our way back to Plum Point in New Windsor where we parked the car," she told him, struggling to form words through her chattering teeth.

"When did you leave the park to go to the island?"

"About four o'clock."

"Who were you with?"

"My boyfriend," she said. They arrived at the gurney where emergency responders were on hand to treat her for hypothermia. To their experienced eyes, they noticed that the rescued woman seemed oddly calm and devoid of emotion.

"What happened when you headed back?" Bedetti asked, trying to collect any information that could help rescuers find Vince

"It got a little rough out. He went over into the water. I lost sight of him because of the waves. I waited for about five minutes after I lost sight of him and called nine-one-one."

"Where is the phone you used to call nine-one-one?"

"It fell in the river when my kayak capsized."

"What was your boyfriend doing in the water?"

"When the kayak overturned, he was clinging to the kayak."

"Did he have a floatation device?" Bedetti asked.

"No."

The police officer heard a cell phone ring and was surprised when no one answered it. "Whose cell phone is ringing?"

The paramedics around Angelika, on the one hand, threw annoyed glances in his direction, as if his question were irrelevant and distracting. Bedetti, on the other hand, thought it was possible that Angelika's phone had not gone in the water after all. The ringtone sounded like it was coming from down by his feet, where Angelika had set down her black bag and life vest.

When Bedetti grabbed the vest, Angelika sat bolt upright and stared at him. He wasn't sure why she was bothered, but her reaction made him uncomfortable. He peeked at the vest and eased it back down on the grass.

"Do you have the keys to the car?" he asked.

"Yes, I have them."

"He definitely doesn't have the keys?"

"No, I have them in the bag."

Bedetti picked it up and handed it to Angelika. She rooted through it and pulled out the keys, showing them off to Bedetti. He put them back and handed the bag and vest to Angelika as she was loaded into the ambulance.

Bedetti watched the ambulance pull out of the park. He thought about returning to the station but decided to follow it to St. Luke's Cornwall Hospital in his own vehicle. He'd learned as a volunteer fireman that every second can mean the difference between life and death and the quicker he obtained information from Angelika the greater the odds that the search for the other kayaker would be successful. He also hoped she was wrong about losing the phone. Locating that device could enable law enforcement to extrapolate from the GPS coordinates to find a more precise spot where Vince went into the water.

Senior Investigator Aniello Moscato of the New York State Police was not on duty on April 19, but when he learned that his team had deployed he went down to the river to help in any way he could. He strongly believed that his role as a supervisor meant he was honor bound to provide support.

When he arrived at the staging area at Gully's, a former Newburgh riverfront restaurant and bar housed in an old barge, the search-and-rescue effort was gaining momentum and resources. In early spring, that portion of the riverside was normally quiet and subdued. The yacht club marina was not up to full speed for the season yet—most of their boaters didn't put their vessels in the water until later that month or early in May. Now police and fire department boats filled the water and helicopters from the New York State Police and Westchester and Rockland County police departments flew overheard, bringing a few people out of their houses on the hill of the opposite shore to check out the increased activity.

Upon arriving at the hospital, Officer Bedetti rummaged through the vehicle he was driving, looking for anything he could use to take notes. All he could find was the piece of card stock stuck in his ticket pack. He grabbed that and headed inside to the emergency room bay. There he found Angelika behind a drawn curtain. A hospital employee was behind it with her, asking questions. Officer Bedetti announced his presence and was invited inside.

Bedetti ran over the same questions again, probing for more detail and jotting down her responses on the back of the card stock. As he talked to her, he picked up the life vest, thinking it was possible that the phone had gotten caught up in the webbing or fallen into a pocket.

"What are you doing?" Angelika asked.

"Inspecting the vest," he said, but when he realized that what he was doing was distracting her attention from the medical personnel he set the vest back down. Then he asked about her cell phone, wanting, at least, to get her phone number to run a trace for the last known coordinates to help locate her boyfriend. He also wanted to know if she'd had it in a box or ziplock that would have protected it from the water if it had fallen in the Hudson.

"No," she said. "I dropped the phone in the water when I overturned my kayak."

Next, Bedetti asked her to describe the kayaks. Angelika not only told him the colors of their crafts but also threw in the dimensions of both. As he was preparing to leave, Angelika asked, "Can you bring me back to my car?"

"It would be better if you stayed here to get treated for whatever they're going to treat for you."

Her shoulders slumped, and she sighed. "Okay."

Bedetti could tell she had grown far less calm than she had been down by the water—she was clearly anxious to get out of there. He handed her his business card and said, "If you need a ride or something after that, call the number for the police department, ask for me, and I'll come by and get you." After leaving the hospital, Bedetti returned to headquarters and wrote his incident report. He accidentally listed the missing person as Victor Viafore.

Senior Investigator Moscato sent Trooper Andrew Freeman of the Montgomery barracks to the hospital to make a determination of the current status of the rescued kayaker. He found her in a bay in the emergency room. He asked if she was okay and offered to make any phone calls for her.

Meanwhile, state police investigator Detective Donald DeQuarto had received a call from Trooper Jason Vidacovich, who informed him that there was a missing kayaker in the Hudson River by the Cornwall Yacht Club and that a rescued female had been taken to the hospital in

Newburgh, where Trooper Freeman had met her. De-Quarto called Freeman and asked to speak to her.

"Can you tell me briefly what happened," he asked

"I was kayaking with my fiancé in the Hudson River, and because of the rough current he overturned his kayak, and I couldn't get to him. I overturned my kayak, too, and they brought me to this hospital," Angelika said.

"I'm on my way there and I'll be there shortly," he said. DeQuarto got to the hospital at 9:30 that evening. When he arrived, Angelika was dressed in hospital-provided garments, her water-soaked clothing stuffed in her bag. She was being processed through discharge and seemed very calm as she filled out release paperwork. He asked if she had any problem coming back to the barracks with him to discuss what had happened.

"No problem," she said.

Trooper Andrew Freeman transported her back to the Montgomery barracks, where DeQuarto joined her. He sat behind his desk and she sat down in a chair beside it. He asked her to run through the events in more detail.

She complied, telling him when she and Vincent had left the mainland and when they'd set out to return after spending a couple of hours on the island shooting photographs.

"What were the colors of your kayaks?"

"I was in a red kayak and Vince was in a blue kayak. Is this all really necessary?" she asked.

"Yes, we have a missing person and we need as many specifics as we can get."

She sighed and began a lengthier description. "We set out to head back to Plum Point—Vince was about fifty feet in front of me. The water was getting really bad and the current was bad. I saw Vince flip out of his kayak and fall into the river. I tried to paddle to him, but I couldn't get to him because the current was pulling me further and

further away. I was exhausted trying to paddle to him.
When he was in the water about five minutes he yelled,
'Call 911.' So, I did. I was telling the dispatcher what happened when the current flipped me into the water. In about
ten minutes, rescue workers came and pulled me out."

"Where were you when Vince flipped out of his kayak?"

"About halfway between Bannerman Island and Plum
Point."

"Was he wearing a life jacket?"

"No, but he had the floatation device he uses as a back-
rest."

DeQuarto wrote up her deposition and handed it to her
to review. "Do you want to change anything with it?"

"No," she said.

"You can sign that if everything is correct."

She signed the document and asked, "Can you take me
back to my car now?"

"Yes," he said.

"Can I call Vince's sister, Laura, first?"

"No problem."

"Can you look up the phone number for me? When I
fell into the water, I saw my phone go into the water. I lost
my phone in the Hudson River and I lost all my contacts
with it."

DeQuarto found the number and gave it to her.

She placed the call to Vince's sister, Laura Rice, just
after 10:00 pm. "Vinny is missing," she said. "We went
kayaking and he went into the water. The police are looking for him."

"Oh my God! Should I come down there? What should
I do?" Laura asked.

"You don't need to. I'm with the officers that will take
me where I need to go."

Hanging up the phone, Laura was stunned and terrified.
She thought about calling her mother but hesitated and

talked to her husband. Laura didn't want to wake Mary Ann Viafore if she was sleeping and didn't want to inflict unnecessary worry on her before they knew the outcome. After all, they reasoned, Vince might be found, hurt but alive, that night. They decided to wait until the next morning to let her know.

Angelika and Investigator DeQuarto walked out to the parking lot, and DeQuarto opened the front passenger door of his car for her. He drove back to her car at Plum Point, arriving there around 11:30.

The searchers were still hard at work. The helicopters zigzagged across the area, shining their bright lights down on the water. People in boats crept through the waves, peering into the darkness and hoping for a glimpse of the missing man. Law enforcement and fire department personnel explored the shoreline searching for Vince or any of his belongings. Scuba dive teams were looking at any unusual objects in the sonar and getting readings on the currents in an attempt to narrow their focus on the most probable location of Vince's body.

Angelika said that she was not sure if Vince had his cell with him or if he'd left it in the car. She and DeQuarto approached the Jeep on different sides, looking in the glove box, under seats, and into crevices, but did not find the phone.

Angelika looked toward the river and yelled, "Vinny!"

Having given up on finding his phone, she walked to her car and told DeQuarto she was going to Laura Rice's house.

"We'll keep searching tonight and I'll call you there if we locate Vince," he told her.

She pulled away from the parking lot with Investigator DeQuarto following her. When they reached 9W, their cars went in opposite directions.

Moments after Angelika and DeQuarto pulled out of

the park, the Westchester County helicopter spotted Vince's blue Fusion kayak—upside down in the river. Montgomery Fire Department secured the vessel; they had to drain a large amount of water out of it to lift it into the boat. Fifteen minutes later, the Rockland County helicopter spotted Angelika's red Clearwater Affinity kayak tangled in downed trees, just south of where Vince's was found. Both were located just north of Plum Point, where they had launched hours ago to paddle to the island. Two Westchester County marine units brought them to the Cornwall Yacht Club along with Vince's blue Pioneer paddle and Angelika's black one. After Investigator DeQuarto took photographs, the kayaks and paddles were transported by the Storm King Fire Department and secured at their nearby facility to await pickup by the state police the next day.

Before the rescue teams called it quits for the night, the state police dive team was advised about the current status of the search. They made plans to be on the scene the next morning at 9:00 when the search resumed.

Just after 2:30 that morning, Troopers Freeman and Vidacovich called local hospitals to see if Vince had been admitted. No one had seen him, but employees were given a description of Vince and asked to call if anyone came in matching his description.

CHAPTER THREE

In accordance with his supervision philosophy, Moscato was on hand when the kayaks and paddles were delivered on Monday, April 20, to the Montgomery barracks by the fire department. He helped with the unloading process, but not being a kayaker, he noted nothing unusual about the condition of the vessels. He did note that the paddles were not assembled for use—they had been broken down, the ring unscrewed, and the two parts separated, in order to fit in the trooper car.

The following day, the search continued over a ten-mile radius, with assistance from a large number of agencies: the Westchester Department of Public Safety; Rockland County Sheriff; fire departments from Cornwall, West Point, Fort Montgomery, Vails Gate, Stony Point, and the City of Newburgh; police departments from Newburgh, Cornwall-on-Hudson, the Town of New Windsor, and the Town of Cornwall, as well as resources from the state police and other agencies. They all worked together from the staging area at Gully's boat dock. Official searchers were joined by civilian volunteers—family and friends of Vince, as well as civic-minded strangers. New York State Troopers handed out flyers on both sides of the river to boaters, hikers, fishermen, everyone spotted in the area. They wanted to talk to anyone who had been in the park between 4:00 and 8:00 pm on April 19.

While the ground searchers scanned the shoreline hoping to find Vince injured but alive, the divers were in the water hunting for a body hung up on a tree branch, a rock, or another underwater impediment. The determination of where the water could have carried his body was complicated by the nature of the Hudson. As it was a tidal river, the directions of flow changed twice a day, dragging any mass first in one direction and then in the other. The dive boat also ran a sonar scan with aerial support by helicopter. The scuba team tried to fine-tune projections of where a body would drift as they searched.

Later on that gray, miserable day, Captain Brendan Casey of the New York State Police stood before a bank of microphones before a crowd of reporters. As he spoke, the falling rain bounced off his hat, punctuating his words. "Our investigation has determined that they brought their personal kayaks down to Plum Point and they launched from there and paddled out to Pollepel Island and were on their way back. Again, reports from the female who was rescued were that they had kayaked in the past, they are experienced kayakers. And it is indeed a bit of a cautionary tale if it is true that they are experienced. People should remember that this time of year, the water is very cold, and the weather can change very quickly, and they should use caution if they are out in the water."

Asked what his challenges were that day, he answered, "We have a state police marine unit in the water with side-scanning sonar. When the water is this rough, it is very difficult to operate, [to] keep your grid line searches uniform and get good readings from the side-scanning sonar. So, they're going to keep pushing a little bit longer but probably have to call it here in a little bit and we'll be back out here tomorrow if the weather turns."

In response to a question about Angelika, he said, "She's obviously upset about her fiancé and not being able to locate him. She has mild hypothermia, so she was taken to the hospital and treated."

Casey then commented on why he thought the accident had happened. "The conditions yesterday changed. It was nice during the day and I think that's what may have lulled them into a sense of complacency. It was a pretty nice day. And then it got cooler and the winds picked up. We're not sure exactly how long she was in the water, but it was long enough for her to start feeling some effects of hypothermia."

Sean Von Clauss, Vince's friend since elementary school, had been in New York City that weekend for a three-day music gig. He returned to his home in Boston on Marathon Monday, April 20. He saw thirty-six missed messages about the accident. Panicked, he went to Angelika's Facebook page to learn more.

Angelika, like many others who have experienced a traumatic event, posted about her ordeal but did not include any details. She started with a positive message thanking everyone for their concern and insisting that "miracles ARE possible." She assured everyone that the authorities were doing everything they could, and she expressed concern that no one else get hurt in the dangerous river. She also pleaded for no questions at that time. She concluded her first post on a hopeful note: "We will find him."

She followed up that entry by updating her profile photo to a romantic black-and-white shot of her and Vince with one of his arms wrapped around her, a hand on her bare shoulder. She also changed her cover picture to one of Vince standing at the end of a narrow pier, holding a glass up in salute. The following day, she shared an image of a candle burning in front of a photo of the two of them on a Carnival Cruise ship, and a photo of Vince holding a glass that she captioned with a wish for a happy "1.7 year anniversary [*sic*]."

That same day, friend Sheri Parte went to the condo where Vince and Angelika lived to offer whatever comfort she could. "I'm freaking out," Sheri told Angelika. She tried to get her friend to open up about the past day's events. "Do you have any photos from when Vinny went missing?" Sheri asked.

"No. I lost my phone. I was talking to nine-one-one and trying to paddle at the same time and a wave swamped the kayak and caused it to capsize," Angelika said in a calm voice.

Sheri could not believe how mellow and matter-of-fact Angelika seemed about the whole situation. She didn't think she could maintain any sense of composure if the same thing had happened to her.

On the twenty-second, Angelika changed her profile picture again—this time to another photo of the couple with both of Vince's arms wrapped around her. She added four more photos to her timeline: a lineup of four silly animal figurines; a snapshot of her cell phone with a photo of her and Vince; a picture of Vince in front of a waterfall; and another of both of them in the same spot. She then posted a message: "I have never felt more grateful in my life than I do now . . . the most sincere thanks to everyone Vince and I know . . . and to those we don't as well!!!"

She changed her profile photo again the next day to one of a flower bed beside the river, with the Bannerman Castle in the background. She also shared a disturbing photograph of herself, alone in a kayak, paddling across the

Hudson River under a dark and ominous sky. She captioned the post: "If only I could have paddled harder, dammit . . ."

Angelika had unsettled Sheri in the immediate aftermath of the accident, but seeing that photograph disturbed her on a deeper level. She told *People* magazine: "It's kind of creepy that she's there alone and it's a stormy day. It was kind of freaky."

In the next few days, suspicions about Angelika loomed larger in the thoughts of more and more people. Soon a great many of them would begin to view Angelika in a less than positive light.

CHAPTER FOUR

The arrested woman whose fiancé was missing in the Hudson River was born Angelika Lipska behind the Iron Curtain in Riga, the capital of the Soviet Socialist Republic of Latvia, on February 27, 1980. In its early history, local factions had controlled the territory, which covered an area a bit larger than West Virginia. During the Middle Ages, its pivotal location on the Baltic Sea made it important territory for other nations to seize, and as a result it was ruled during different periods by Germany, Poland, Lithuania, Sweden, and finally Russia. During the reign of the Tsars, Peter the Great married a Latvian woman who, upon his death, ruled over all of Russia as Catherine I.

Latvia declared its independence in 1918 and maintained it until 1940 when the Soviets overran their nation and annexed it as a Communist state. A year later, Nazi troops marched the streets, which continued until 1944, when Soviet forces routed the Germans and regained control. After the war, the USSR built up the industrial base of the country to the point that there were not enough Latvians to fill all the jobs created. This called for the immigration of a large number of Russians into Latvia. Angelika's ancestors were part of this new ethnic Russian population that soon equaled the population of native-born. The official language became Russian, which was required for all official transactions and for admission into institutes of higher learning.

By the time Angelika was born, public displays by enthusiastic crowds in support of the Soviet regime were ordered on all anniversaries of prominent dates in the Russian revolutionary calendar. Latvians rallied as required, but unrest was building in the populace as they faced increasing shortages of food and consumer goods. The earliest signs of rebellion against Soviet authority were seen in a thriving black market and through the prevalent elevations in work absenteeism and in escalating alcoholism.

Mikhail Gorbachev, leader of the USSR, introduced the political and economic reforms known as glasnost and perestroika midway through the first decade of the young girl's life. She was seven years old in the summer of 1987 when large demonstrations erupted in Riga at the Freedom Monument, to commemorate the mass deportation of more than forty-three thousand native Latvians to Siberia in June 1941. The disruption was the catalyst for the formation of the Popular Front of Latvia.

In November, on Independence Day 1989, half a million Latvians gathered to protest again in Riga. These displays of resistance eventually led to the victory of the pro-independence party in March 1990.

That was a heady year in Latvia. In March, an election was held for the first time in decades that allowed the participation of multiple political parties. The Republic of Latvia established a transition period that would lead to a full parliamentary democracy. On May 4, the 1940 annexation of the Republic of Latvia was declared illegal, unconstitutional, and against the will of the people. The republic reinstated a portion of the 1922 constitution. Their relationship with the Soviet Union reverted to the conditions of the 1920 treaty, in which the Soviets had recognized the independence of Latvia "for all time." May 4 remains a national holiday throughout Latvia, known as Independence Restoration Day.

On May 7, Soviet tanks and other armored vehicles rolled through Riga to intimidate the citizens with a show of military strength. Moscow made several attempts to stop the independence of the three Baltic States—Latvia, Estonia, and Lithuania. Nonetheless, under Premier Mikhail Gorbachev and his perestroika policy, all of them regained their independence before the total dissolution of the Soviet Socialist Republics in 1991.

In addition to the tumult facing her country, Angelika's personal life was chaotic and mired in poverty. Her mother worked hard at cleaning other people's houses, while at home there was no hot running water. At a young age, Angelika realized that if she was going to have a better life she needed to make decisions and take actions to create a change in her circumstances.

Riga, a thriving port for centuries, was the industrial, shipping, and cultural center of Latvia. The city is considered by many to be the Art Nouveau capital of northern Europe, with elegant and evocative architecture dotting the town center. At the time of Angelika's birth, Riga boasted a population of three-quarters of a million.

The preteen Angelika and her family, along with all citizens of their small Baltic country, were liberated from the shroud of totalitarian government in 1991. New opportunities and horizons opened in a rush. Liberty did not lift the family from the bottom of the economic barrel, but it did strengthen and elevate the power of the young girl's dreams.

Angelika found comfort in photography, documenting the beauty of the great forests and majestic beaches of her native land. For entertainment, she learned to play guitar and sing popular Western songs. She escaped her hectic reality by indulging in an imagined new life in the United States one day.

Angelika grabbed that opportunity with desperate urgency when she turned twenty. She sought and obtained a visa to emigrate to America through a position as a nanny for a prominent family in Greenwich, Connecticut. When she said good-bye to her mother, she only planned to stay for one short year. Life in the United States, however, exceeded her childhood dreams, and she extended her stay.

Less than eighteen months after the barely five-foot-tall young woman had started her position, there was a problem with the heating and cooling system in the family's home. A repair company was called to repair it, and Shawn Maloney arrived on the doorstep.

After a whirlwind romance, Shawn and Angelika were married, but it lasted barely a year and ended in 2003. Shawn held no grudges about the relationship, saying that they were simply too young and moved too quickly into commitment.

While with Shawn, the now-21-year-old Angelika left her nanny job and started working as a bartender. She alternated between that and waitressing jobs up to and after the breakup. She had a natural knack for remembering names, which served her well in both positions. She played guitar and sang onstage when she was off duty, as a solo act or accompanying local bands. However, she had a problem with authority. Because of that, she changed working situations a lot, usually because she would lose her temper in a staff meeting and end up unemployed. Through it all, though, she worked on developing her skills as a photographer, focusing on animals, landscapes, or inanimate objects. She rarely ever took pictures of people.

Soon after her marriage ended, Angelika met Richard Graswald. He was the owner of North Eastern Decorative Concrete, a business that incorporated his knowledge and experience with concrete and his natural creative talents. After a short period of dating, they married and moved to Shelton, Connecticut. She quit her restaurant job and focused on her photography for a while, entering and occasionally winning competitions, including a first- and third-place finish in the national KODAK Gallery Awards. Her photographs, along with those of the other winners, went on a world tour with a stop in New York City. In addition, one of her shots made it into an edition of Petersen photography guides. She also studied at a community college, graduating with honors in English.

Her second marriage, too, was destined to be a short-term relationship. In the fall of 2008, Angelika started a temporary job with a Connecticut-based company in Hyde Park, New York, creating a digital record of the historical documents and photographs at the Franklin D. Roosevelt Presidential Library and Museum. Monday through Friday, her days were filled with endless scanning. For months, she'd return to her home and Richard each weekend. However, she was growing bored with the relationship, claiming that after the wedding they no longer had sex.

On weekday nights, she looked for relaxation and excitement by immersing herself in the rich music scene at the Poughkeepsie area bars. Ken Veltz had energized that world when he started providing free live music in his Listening Room at Whistling Willie's American Grill. He pulled in the Brooklyn musicians he knew as well as performers visiting from Los Angeles. One frequent guest was

Tony Garnier, longtime bassist and musical director for Bob Dylan. More than two hundred musicians participated in his Listening Room performance rounds in the two short years of its existence, from December 2007 to November 2009.

After work at the FDR library on November 5, 2008, Angelika stopped by Mahoney's Irish Pub. Mike Colvin, a former on-air personality for WPDH, was the Wednesday evening DJ for karaoke night. Angelika stepped up for three songs, including one of her favorites, "Objection" by Shakira.

She and Mike chatted while she was waiting to take the stage. He was intrigued by her accent and attracted to her upbeat personality. By the time Mike's shift was over, the two of them were upstairs making out. She came back to the pub several times that month, and Mike was always glad to see her again. It was the start of a new relationship.

CHAPTER FIVE

Mike was a well-known area DJ. He'd started his career at the classic rock station WDPH in 1997. His signature event, the Roof-A-Thon, was an annual fifty-one-hour broadcast from the roof of the 7-Eleven in Wappingers Falls, raising money for the Lower Hudson Valley and Fairfield County chapter of the Muscular Dystrophy Association. He'd started out as a volunteer, but soon he was the co-host, along with his "Coop and Mikey" morning show partner, Mark Cooper.

In August 2003, Mike and Mark kicked off the nineteenth annual Roof-A-Thon. By the time it ended, they'd raised $127,000. The next day, Mark's wife gave birth to their son: Thomas. The radio station sent flowers with a note that read: "Welcome, Thomas, to the home of Rock 'n' Roll."

Nine short days after that, station management asked Mike and Mark to attend a meeting after their on-air shift. When they arrived, they were fired for a drop in their ratings and a change in the station's format. So much for their successful fundraiser—so much for the oft-repeated "We are family" phrase—the duo was tossed out like yester-day's trash.

Mike had already started a separate DJ business, play-ing music at bars and pubs as well as weddings and other social occasions. He knew he'd be able to make it finan-cially, but he worried about his partner, who'd just become a father.

It took three years, but Mark Cooper was eventually hired back as a co-host of the morning show at WPDH in September 2006. Over the years, Mike built up his pro-fessional DJ business to a success that enabled him to vol-unteer his services to a variety of charitable organizations.

Mike was outside hanging Christmas lights on the Friday after Thanksgiving 2008 when Angelika called and said, "I'm leaving Richard." He thought it was a bit odd that she'd contacted him with the news. It made more sense a couple of days later when she showed up at his doorstep, suitcase in hand: "I don't have a place to live. I'm moving in with you."

Mike had never made that offer to her and, in fact, had never made any kind of commitment to Angelika. None-theless, he was an easygoing guy and didn't interfere with her plans. She moved right into his place.

Everything went well with the new arrangement, at first. Angelika had to be at the presidential library each weekday morning, and his work kept him out until 4:00 am most nights. They slept side by side for a few hours each night, often engaging in physical intimacy, but didn't have much time for other forms of social interaction.

On December 2, Mike made a guest appearance with his former radio partner on a special anniversary show, re-counting the ten years they'd spent on the air together. Angelika came along to show her support and enjoy the music. While they were out, Richard Graswald showed up at Mike's home. He took pictures of the exterior of the house and posted them on Facebook with comments about Angelika, mocking the fact that she lived there now and had left him for what Richard obviously saw as an inferior situation.

Mike said that Richard continued to escalate the situation after those posts, leaving messages on Mike's phone, calling him names like "scumbag." Soon he'd taken it up another notch by making flat-out threats. Mike was disturbed enough to file a complaint with the police. More than once, Mike asked himself, "What the hell am I doing with this chick?" But still, he avoided confrontation and did nothing to change the situation.

When Angelika learned Richard was going to Florida, she took matters into her own hands. She borrowed an SUV from a friend, drove to Connecticut, and broke into Richard's home. No one could have blamed her if she'd merely retrieved her own belongings, but she took it much further. She cleaned out the house, packing the car until it couldn't hold any more. When she returned to Poughkeepsie, Mike was shocked at what she'd taken—tools she didn't know how to use, garage materials she had no reason to use, and even every single roll of toilet paper she could find.

"It's one thing to take your clothes and stuff, but this is all his stuff. It isn't right," Mike told her. All his objections fell on deaf ears. "You couldn't tell Angelika anything—you could not tell her right from wrong," Mike reflected.

Mike tried to cajole her to do the right thing, but to no avail. Richard, too, asked her to return his belongings, but in the end, he had to take her to court with an itemized list to retrieve his possessions. Their divorce was finalized the following year.

At the end of January 2009, Angelika's temporary job

came to an end and she lost the company car she had used to travel there and back. Unemployed, she had more time and energy to go with Mike to his DJ gigs and social events. Mike introduced her to Sorluna de Butterfly, one of his close friends whom they'd run into at Mahoney's Irish Pub. Mike, Sorluna said, liked to show off Angelika, wanting his friends to admire her. Sorluna thought Angelika was a very positive and happy person and gladly accepted her as a friend, too. When it was apparent that the two women got along, Sorluna claimed that Mike suggested that she join him and Angelika in a threesome. Although this was a common desire among Hudson Valley men according to Sorluna, the idea seemed odd to her since Angelika was half her age.

Although Mike seemed to like having Angelika around as arm candy, he complained that she spent all her time on his couch and exhibited no enthusiasm to find another job. This attitude, he said later, had a negative impact on the already shallow and shaky relationship.

Finally, Mike put his foot down—living with her was one thing; supporting her was another. He spent five thousand dollars on a used Hyundai Elantra and told her she had to get a job. When she didn't make the effort, he found a job for her as a waitress and bartender at Mahoney's Casperkill Golf Club.

Angelika was a contentious employee. She was often late to work, even though she didn't need to get there until 11:00 in the morning. She did not take criticism well and wanted to do things her way instead of following instructions. "When she didn't get what she felt she had a right to, there was a spiteful side to her," Mike said. He described those instances as "her Russian coming out."

It didn't take long before she was fired from Mahoney's, but she did bounce to a different position at the Silver

Spoon Cafe, a restaurant on Main Street in Cold Spring known for its burgers, vegetarian options, and seven flavors of hot chocolate. It was there that she met Joel Goss, a musician, writer, director, and producer. He introduced her to the performers in his circle. Soon she was taking the stage with many of them to sing backup.

Joel saw her as a cute little blonde with a delightful accent whose habit of hanging around the bar to listen to music after work brought a lot of attention to her. As a result, men constantly hit on her. He thought she handled those encounters well, avoiding conflict and hard feelings.

One night, he saw a couple of guys pestering her, asking to buy her drinks. She told them, "You can buy me a drink if you drink one, too."

Joel sidled up to her and said, "You think you can hold your liquor better than they can and you don't want them to think you owe them something at the end of the evening, right?"

Angelika lowered her head. When she lifted her chin, she grinned and said, "Yes."

When Angelika lost her job at Silver Spoon, she moved up the street to Joel's regular hang-out, Whistling Willie's American Grill, with its vintage mahogany bar and 150-year history. There she continued to perform backup for other artists including Joel, trumpeter David Dash, and singer/songwriter Derek Dempsey.

Joel appreciated her photography and talked to Angelika frequently about it. When her camera was stolen out of her car one night, he gave her his old camera so that she could keep shooting. Joel came to her rescue again, when she was having technical trouble with her photo-editing software, downloading his program onto her laptop.

Another facet of Angelika that interested Joel was her old-world sense that spirits were always roaming among us. He thought it natural that she'd wound up in the Hudson Valley, the home of the Headless Horseman and generations of ghost stories in every village.

One snowy evening, Angelika visited Joel and his family at their home. She was instantly besotted with the betta fish Joel's son owned. She stood in front of the aquarium staring at it for a long stretch of time. When Joel approached her, she said, "I can feel a lot of ghosts in your house."

"Does that bother you?" he asked.

"No." She vigorously shook her head. "Not at all, except for one of them. He is over in that corner," she said, pointing across the room. "I won't go near that corner. He is angry or upset and I don't want to get near him."

Angelika's stint at Whistling Willie's lasted eighteen months—the longevity had more to do with the patience and forgiveness of her employer than with her performance. Her boss was pleased that although she had a pronounced accent, she had no trouble at all speaking and understanding English as a bartender and waitress. Her breadth of comprehension was vast and her perception of nuance in the language exceeded that of even some native speakers.

She aggravated her employer, though, with her lack of work ethic. She hid downstairs to avoid working, conducted leisurely phone calls to get out of cleaning up, and often refused to accept table assignments when she wanted to leave early.

However, Angelika was quick to pursue platonic friendships with customers and coworkers. She had a knack for making and keeping friends with ease. "She could walk into a roomful of strangers and know everyone's name by the time she left," Mike said. Coworkers and regular customers sought her out, and she fostered a sense of belonging in the community.

In the few years she'd spent in the United States, she'd been thoroughly Americanized. The customs of her adopted country quickly became second nature to her—even making her a big football fan. She loved cheering the chosen team at Mike's football parties and worked hard at being a great hostess. But Mike was still bothered by her temper. Her angry moments were more extreme than those of anyone else he'd ever encountered.

Angelika visited Latvia every two years. As 2010 was an off year, her younger sister Jelena visited her and stayed in Mike's home. Mike said that while there Jelena played guitar but didn't speak very often.

In May 2010, Mike and friends were making their annual trek to the Fest for Beatles Fans in New Jersey. Founded in 1974, the event is billed as the "Original and Longest Running Beatles Celebration."

After a daylong party in the hotel room, complete with free-flowing alcohol, Mike suffered the frequent side effect of those circumstances that night. He wasn't able to perform sexually. Most women blew those occasional failures off or blamed themselves, but not Angelika. She grew furious. She felt insulted and no longer considered Mike a real man.

She refused to sleep in the same bed with Mike and moved all of her clothing and belongings into the guest room after they returned to Poughkeepsie. The intimate part of their life was over. At work, she sought romantic relationships with the same vigor that she'd employed in making friends. She was casual in dispensing her sexual favors. She got busy looking for a male replacement for Mike, even dating one 60-year-old patron.

CHAPTER SIX

Angelika seemed incapable of forming a lasting relationship with a man. It was as if she needed a male in her life to feel complete but really didn't like them all that much. She expected them to support her financially, be in sync with her sexual appetites, and do everything her way. The moment she didn't get precisely what she wanted, when she wanted it, she saw her partner of the moment as more of a nuisance than an asset. When that happened, she usually was off trolling for a new man without any downtime.

Before long, Angelika met a man named Pat. At home, she gushed about him to Mike. They had a lot in common. First and foremost, he, too, was a photographer. She was also excited that Pat owned a kayak and loved to hear her talk about her experiences kayaking on the Baltic Sea in Latvia and on Lake Zoar in Connecticut.

She spent an increasing amount of time with Pat, with them hanging out and going on photo shoots together. Pat was the photographer of the picture that raised a lot of eyebrows when Angelika later posted it on Facebook while Vince was missing—the shot of her in a kayak on the Hudson River, under an ominous sky.

When Pat and Angelika decided to live together, Pat went to Mahoney's to talk to Mike about their plans. Mike was polite and didn't say what he was really thinking, but he was relieved that, at last, someone was taking Angelika off his hands.

Pat was living with his sister at the time and moved Angelika into her house with him. His sister said there was no way that his girlfriend could live there, too, and she kicked Pat out on the street. The couple ended up settling in a tent on the Highland side of the Hudson River.

Angelika and Mike's breakup flowed along in an amicable fashion, up to the point when Mike made a demand. Everything went sideways when he insisted that she return the Hyundai Elantra—the insurance was in his name and he wasn't comfortable letting her continue to drive it. Angelika was furious and wanted to get back at Mike in some way. On July 4, 2010, she drove to Mike's house, accompanied by Pat in his car, to return the Hyundai and pick up her belongings. Mike waited patiently as she gathered her things, even though he was due at work. He certainly didn't want to leave her alone in his house, knowing what she'd done to Richard Graswald.

When she finished packing up her stuff, she said, "I want the cat," referring to Myetka, a black cat with white spots given to the couple by Mike's sister.

"You're living in a tent," Mike said. "There's no way you can take care of a cat."

"I want the cat," she insisted.

"No way are you taking our cat to a tent on the Hudson River."

"No!" she shouted, stomping her foot. "If you don't let

me have the cat, I'll break into the house and take it." She lay down on the driveway right behind Mike's car, daring him to run over her.

Mike tried to get her to move, but she refused. He looked to Pat, hoping for some assistance. But Pat just sat in his car, looking shocked and stunned by the drama unfolding over the custody of the animal.

Finally, Mike relented. If he hadn't, he knew she would stay there and make him late to work. He watched her drive away with Myetka, hoping the cat would be okay. He was still unnerved, however, by her threat of a break-in. The next day, he had a security system installed.

He was right about the difficulty of caring for a cat when your home was a tent. Three or four days later, Angelika returned, cat in tow. She begrudgingly admitted that she couldn't keep Myetka.

Rodney Van Dunk, a friend of Angelika's, told the media that in the aftermath of leaving Mike she spent a lot of time at a bar, which he said was sometimes frequented by swingers just over the state line in New Jersey. She was a weekly regular who arrived with three or four girls, all dressed up to meet men, he claimed: "She was like a vulture looking for a sugar daddy."

It seemed that Angelika didn't look at it that way. She appeared to want the emotional and financial security of a committed relationship with a man she could love. With that mind-set, she was ready to fall for the charismatic Vincent Viafore when he came into her life. With gorgeous blue eyes and crazy dance moves that made everyone laugh, Vince checked all the boxes.

CHAPTER SEVEN

Mary Ann Pavone and Vincent T. Viafore both lived in the Bronx and worked in Manhattan. Vincent had just gotten out of the army when he met Mary Ann at a Saturday night dance in 1962. "We were just two crazy teenagers who eloped," Mary said of their whirlwind romance. They had a proper wedding in a church afterwards to keep her parents happy.

A year later, their first child was born: a daughter they named Laura. Vincent Alexander Viafore was the second child born to the couple in Bronxville, New York, on August 22, 1968. Laura was almost in kindergarten when Vince stole away her only-child status. In 1970, the family moved to Dutchess County and settled in Wappingers Falls, a village that had experienced explosive growth in the preceding decade. Wappingers Creek ran through the 1.2-acre community and continued flowing for about two miles before its convergence with the Hudson River.

The family moved into a new development in a home on Granger Place, in a quiet middle-class neighborhood of rolling hills, cookie-cutter homes, and big yards for play.

Their small ranch house had green aluminum siding and a large aboveground pool in the backyard enclosed by a chain-link fence. After only knowing city life, when Vince first arrived at his new home he was intimidated by the yard. He was afraid to walk on the grass. Their property abutted a nice stretch of woods that scared him, too, at first, but when he grew a little older he'd spent hours playing with friends there.

Every Sunday, the family went to church and brought home bagels. During football season, they'd all gather in front of the television to watch the games. Each member of the family had their own team: Dad was a Pittsburgh Steelers fan, Mom rooted for the Miami Dolphins, Laura loved the New York Jets, and Vince's team was the Dallas Cowboys.

Vince's maternal relatives were of Italian or Sicilian ancestry, and his paternal ancestry was a mix—his grandmother was Polish and his grandfather Italian. With that background, pasta was a big part of the family menu. It was served every Sunday with sauce that in the Italian tradition was called gravy. Vince's maternal grandmother, who lived in Yonkers, looked after him whenever his mother was working. He spent Christmases with his paternal grandmother, who lived in Lakeville, Connecticut.

In October of 1976, Vinny's parents started a business called Construction Layout Men. Two years later, they got a DBA and started operating under the name Ridgewood Construction.

Childhood friend Stacy Speirs met Vinny when they were both three years old and attended story time at a local day care. The two of them hit it off right away, and the friendship would be formative for both of them throughout adolescence. "Vinny was always a very mischievous boy," Stacy remembered. She said that he was "hell on wheels" riding his Big Wheel, always ready to go down

steeper ramps at higher speeds and often ending up with
cuts, scrapes, and bruises for his recklessness.

They lived less than two blocks apart in the neighborhood of Rockingham Farms. Vinny and Stacy went back
and forth from each other's homes constantly. As it was a
new neighborhood, the trees hadn't had enough time to
grow and block the view between houses. When Stacy
headed to Vince's, her mother would call Vince's mom and
let her know her daughter was on the way. Mrs. Viafore
would watch out the window for her arrival. She did the
same when Vince went to the Speirs home.

For a decade, Stacy and Vinny would attend each other's
birthday parties. Because Stacy's birthday was near Halloween, her mother hosted a costume party for her each
year. When Stacy was eight years old, she chose a vampire
costume for the celebration. When Vinny arrived, he was
dressed in the same costume. Stacy burst into tears. She
wanted to be the only vampire at the party. Vinny, seeing
her distress, immediately took off his costume and said,
"You be the vampire, I'll just be me."

Growing up, Vince was an altar boy and an avid par-
ticipant in Boy Scouts, in part because of his dad. Vince's
father came with him on overnight camp-outs and helped
build the small cars to race on the little tracks. He met lifelong friend Kevin Beisswinger at Scouts. They also
played on the same neighborhood Pop Warner football
team, went to the same schools, and were part of the same
bowling league.

Stacy fondly recalled growing up in a neighborhood where
all the kids could ride bicycles without worry and everybody knew everyone. She said that most of the residents
were transplants from New York City and had created the
"Norman Rockwell" environment they'd sought out when

they fled to the suburbs. Gena Vanzillota, who also grew up in the community with Vince, told the *New York Times:* "Half the neighborhood was Italian, the other half was Irish. It was almost like a little Bronx or Yonkers." In warm weather, the neighborhood kids staged "World Series" wiffle-ball tournaments and went hunting for crawfish in the stream. In the fall, they held "Halloween Wars"—a battle between the Rockingham Farms community and the development next to theirs called Angel Brook. Vince lived on the street that connected the two neighborhoods. As a result, he had friends on both sides of the playful conflict. For the most part, he took the side of the neighborhood where he lived, but he couldn't resist joining his Angel Brook friends for some egg, shaving cream, and toilet paper attacks on Rockingham Farms homes from time to time.

Winter drove the kids inside for Monopoly and other board games in the basement. As Vince and Stacy grew up, their feelings for each other evolved. Vince was Stacy's first crush, she admitted. One night down in the cellar, Vince kept trying to get up the nerve to kiss Stacy, but he was so shy that he kept backing down. Stacy took matters into her own hands and initiated the kiss. It was her first real kiss.

After eighth grade, Vince followed his sister, Laura, to Roy C. Ketcham High School, while Stacy stayed in the Catholic school system. His high school friends described him as gregarious, a popular member of the wrestling team who would flit from table to table in the cafeteria like a "social butterfly."

Even though their paths no longer crossed very often, Vince was still there for Stacy in times of need. Ugly rumors began to spread through the gossip mill at Stacy's parochial high school. Stacey was labeled a "slut" and shunned by many people who she had thought were friends. Stacy's world was crushed, and she felt humiliated.

When the stories eventually reached the public high school, Vince didn't believe a word of the vicious tales. He sought out Stacy to tell her, "I don't believe what they're saying about you." That simple statement healed a lot of Stacy's pain, letting her know she was not alone. Vince took it even further, defending his old friend and her reputation to everyone who spoke a harsh word against her.

Vince graduated in 1986. In the yearbook, next to his photo, his personal message read: "When the summer is gone, and school is almost on, pass the brew around, and you'll get through safe and sound." He had no idea of what he wanted to do with his life after college. He attended Dutchess County Community College for a year before leaving. He held a couple of jobs for a short time until his father connected him to a job with engineering and design firm Parsons Brinckerhoff, which contracted with the New York State Office of General Services Design and Construction Department. He continued his education while he worked, taking classes that helped him advance in his career. Vince worked as a Certified Code Enforcement Official, inspecting fire alarm systems and elevators, and later as a Project Manager. He would work at Parsons Brinckerhoff until his death.

CHAPTER EIGHT

By 1990, Vince's parents had separated and Mary Ann's financial problems had begun. She obtained her estranged husband's power of attorney and arranged for a fifty-thousand-dollar second mortgage on the family home. On September 30, 1994, Mary Ann filed an uncontested divorce petition. The marriage was dissolved a month and a half later.

While his parents' marriage was ending, Vince began dating a woman named Susan Giordano in the early nineties. Soon they were married, but, almost as if his parents' troubles were foreshadowing his own life, Susan filed for divorce in February of 1997.

"As a married couple they were like oil and water," Mary Ann said. "Susan was a fiery little thing, but I liked her." After splitting up, the two remained friends, both on Facebook and in real life. When Susan's mother passed away, Vince supported Susan as if they were still married, assisting with the preparations for the funeral.

On January 9, 1999, Vince remarried—this time to Suzanne Carson. Suzanne had grown up in the same Wappingers Falls neighborhood as Vince, but since she was two years younger—a big difference to little kids—their paths had never crossed.

Suzanne was in college when they wed, changing her major to nursing soon after and earning her R.N. The couple began their life together on Drum Court in Wappingers Falls. During the warm-weather months, they frequently went kayaking. They often thought about attempting a crossing of the Hudson River, but Vince believed it was too dangerous.

On July 6, 2001, Vinny's father, now living in New Jersey, passed away at the young age of 62. In February 2004, Vinny and Suzanne moved a small distance north when they purchased a home in the Fox Hill Condominiums complex in the Town of Poughkeepsie. The name Poughkeepsie often generated confusion to those unfamiliar with the area because there are two of them and both hug the Hudson River. The geographically smaller City of Poughkeepsie had a population of nearly thirty-three thousand. Wrapping around the City on three sides is the Town of Poughkeepsie, with over forty-three thousand residents, and home to Vassar College, one of the Seven Sisters of the Ivy League.

In February 2009, Vince and Suzanne moved to Pleasant Valley, just north of the city of Poughkeepsie, after purchasing a gorgeous home with an in-ground pool, a sunroom, a lovely kitchen with granite countertops, and four bedrooms.

But Vince's indulgences and generosity to friends were beginning to cripple him financially. He often treated friends to drinks at a bar and gave away his own money and property to those in need. His 2005 Jeep Grand Cherokee and his 2006 Stingray boat were repossessed, and his credit card debt neared eighty thousand dollars. Vince filed for a Chapter 13 bankruptcy on November 29, 2010.

Again, it was as if he were following his parents' path. His mother was in the middle of Chapter 7 proceedings, having begun her ordeal two years earlier. Her finances were complicated by a judgement against her for unpaid New York State real estate and personal property taxes in excess of five thousand dollars. Vince's situation was wrapped up more quickly than his mother's, and his file was closed in February 2012.

His troubles were not over, however. In a mutual decision, Sue and Vince both moved in and out of the house a couple of times, one living in an apartment while the other stayed in the home they owned. Suzanne filed for divorce in November 2012. The couple wanted different things out of life and, as his mother reflected, "Vinny was very stubborn." Suzanne bought out his share of the marital home and their marriage was dissolved on March 20, 2013.

After he left his house for the last time, Vinny moved in with a platonic friend, Amanda Bopp. "He was the most genuine, soulful, funniest best friend I'll ever have," she remembered.

One October, Amanda flew out to California to see a friend and attend a Halloween party. On the way back, Vince planned to meet her in Las Vegas. However, Vince's plans were disrupted by Hurricane Sandy. Because of its second landfall in the Northeast, his flight was canceled. He was distressed at the prospect of Amanda being out in Las Vegas all alone—he did not think it was a safe place for a single woman. He booked three different substitute flights, determined to get out there at all costs. His gamble paid off. He arrived in "Sin City" to accompany Amanda. As everyone said, Vince never left anyone hanging.

The caring and concern he demonstrated with others was a guiding principle of Vince's life. He never missed a family celebration on the holidays or other important occasions. He cultivated a particularly close relationship with his only nephew, Michael Rice. When Michael was young, he and Vince played sports together. As adults, Vince was like a big brother to his nephew. They'd go out to Mahoney's Irish Pub and other venues together. For his family and friends, Vince was a constant.

While Vince was working through the red tape of his legal dilemmas, he found respite in running. The Walkway Over the Hudson was one of his favorite routes once it opened to the public on October 3, 2009, part of the four-hundred-year anniversary commemorations of Henry Hudson's exploration of the river that defined the area.

Formerly the Poughkeepsie-Highland Railroad Bridge, the bridge had been hailed as the eighth wonder of the world in 1888 when the 1.25-mile span was first completed. But after it caught fire in 1974 and was subsequently abandoned by railroad traffic, it became a derelict eyesore. Estimates to demolish the structure soared past $40 million. However, someone had a better idea—for $5 or $6 million, the bridge could be resurrected as a walking path.

Fundraisers for the Walkway foundation kicked off the effort. Engineers, divers, and construction workers followed through on the plans. The effort took nineteen years, but the end result was a majestic midair pathway floating twenty-one stories above the beautiful and powerful river. Vince loved every foot of it.

He also ran competitively. In the Dutchess County Classic five-kilometer marathon in Freedom Plains in September 2012, he finished with a time of 25:46:90, placing him in the top half of all racers.

Throughout all the chaos in Vince's life, Sean Von Clauss remained his friend and an active part of his social circle. Vinny often announced his arrival at a party with a robust shout of, "Crazy Clauss is in the house!"

But their relationship was deeper than their party

patter made it seem. They were both there for each other when it counted. Sean said, "Vinny was an amazing person: always the life of the party and yet could stop people from doing stupid things. He made me a better person."

One evening, their elementary school gang met up at Billy Joe's Ribs in Newburgh. After a great night of laughter, catching up, and reminiscing on the good old days, Vince stopped Sean in the parking lot. "Hey, crazy Clauss, come here."

Vince then brought up the taboo subject of Sean's estrangement from his daughter. Sean had previously been married to a woman six years older than him who came from an affluent family. As a musician, Sean was on the road for performances more than he was at home. He fell into the rock 'n' roll lifestyle of hard partying and late nights. His wife finally had enough. She gave Sean an ultimatum: give up playing music or give up your family.

Sean said he thought that it was an idle threat, until the day he came home from a tour and his key wouldn't work in the door. She'd changed all the locks. His ex-wife gained full custody in a divorce and, according to Sean, it was impossible for him to have visitation. He told Vinny the last time he'd seen his daughter, she was three years old.

Vince knew the history and also knew that Sean didn't like to talk about it. However, he felt that it was about time to do so. "I'm proud of you, man," Vince told him. "You've come a long way from your rock-star, long-hair, sex, drugs, and rock 'n' roll days. I'm so happy you're clean and sober and are back playing music. You have a natural talent and an amazing voice. But, my brother, you need to get your daughter back in your life. I know it's a sore subject and you refuse to talk about it, but you have to complete your journey and get her back in your life."

Big, bad Sean, with tears rolling down his face, wrapped his friend in a bear hug and said, "I love ya, brother." Sean wasn't just moved in the moment. Vince inspired him to reengage with his daughter, and together they began to rebuild their relationship.

Sean had met Angelika through his career as a musician. He was performing at a St. Columba Catholic School get-together in early 2013 when Angelika and Vince first saw each other. Sean introduced the two, but Vince was in the purgatory of divorce proceedings at the time and nothing more came of their encounter.

His marriage to Suzanne officially ended on March 20, 2013, and all that was past history by September 22 of that year, when Vince showed up at Mahoney's Irish Pub to drink beer and hang with friends as they watched the much-anticipated New York Jets–Buffalo Bills football game. Mike Colvin was there, too. His former radio partner, Mark Cooper, had recently passed away at the age of 49. He left behind Thomas, his now-10-year-old son.

That afternoon, Mike was DJing a fundraiser to raise money for the boy's education. Angelika was there taking photographs of the event. This time, Vinny could focus on the women around him and he was smitten by the tiny energetic, cheerful woman with the cute accent. The instant attraction was mutual

Although Vince was eleven years older than Angelika, they had a lot of the same interests. They both loved kayaking and were always ready to participate in outdoor sports and athletic activities. Both were fond of gourmet cooking and wine. They also found common ground in their romantic pasts, with two marriages and two divorces apiece. Before parting ways that evening, the two made plans for their first date.

CHAPTER NINE

To many people, Angelika and Vince seemed to have fallen deeply in love. Sean Von Clauss was one of them. He said that they would slow dance whenever he performed "Shama Lama Ding Dong" at his shows. "They were always in love—singing, dancing, holding. They were always together." Vince, he said, "was thrilled that he found his soul mate." Friend Meghan Avezzano told the *Poughkeepsie Journal* that she thought they were "the perfect couple. I never saw any fighting. He always had his arm around her. They were lovey-dovey."

When they met, Vince was living in a friend's apartment and Angelika had a flat with mold problems. Soon Vince found a tan brick condo on Cherry Hill Drive in the town of Poughkeepsie. Though the relationship was steady, his friends were surprised when, in early October, Angelika moved in with him. A month after she moved in, Vince added her as the primary beneficiary on his three insurance policies—one life insurance policy through his employer with Zurich American Insurance and the life and accidental death policies he'd purchased on his own because of the riskiness of some of his work. Putting her name on the policies seemed to be a radical move so early on in their relationship. To Vince, however, it was logical. Angelika needed health coverage. To be able to provide it through his job, he had to establish that she was his domestic partner. One of the prerequisites for that was adding her as a beneficiary to his life insurance.

After his fourteen-year-long marriage to Suzanne ended, Vince had vowed to everyone who would listen that he was going to be a single man for a long time. The rapid advancement of his romance with Angelika was a shocker.

By then, Angelika was working at a sports bar, Grand Centro Grill. When she wasn't working, she'd accompany Vince to his weekly billiards and volleyball tournaments. Although she enjoyed going out and meeting his friends, Angelika said she was happiest during their time alone together.

Vince's intentions were serious enough that he wanted his sister and her husband, Kevin, to meet Angelika. He invited them to dinner at Grand Centro Grill. Because his sister had teased him about his proclivity to date women in their twenties, he told her, "I'm dating a girl and you'll be happy because she's thirty-four."

Vince also exhibited the seriousness of his commitment by learning Angelika's native language. He studied Russian books and dictionaries and asked her about words and grammar. Every weekend morning, over morning coffee, he devoted time to developing his language skills. The two even had Russian nicknames for each other. Angelika called him *yozhik*, meaning "hedgehog," for the texture of his hair. He called her *svinka* or "piggy".

In December 2013, the couple went on a ten-day cruise from New York City down to the Bahamas. They went ashore at Cape Canaveral and took an excursion to Sea

World in Orlando, Florida. In the Bahamas, they disembarked at Nassau and visited a private island. The tropical days of play and revelry and the moonlit nights staring out to sea together cemented their commitment to the relationship.

But Vince, like many men, was not happy about his girlfriend working in a bar. Sean Von Clauss and Vince talked to her about quitting her bartending job and studying to get her real estate license. Angelika liked the idea and decided to quit. Now that she wasn't working, she had time to do volunteer gardening at the grounds on Bannerman Island, as well as more time to help out with the menagerie at the Shepherd's View Animal Sanctuary in Cold Spring, a shelter for cats, dogs, birds, bunnies, goats, sheep, and more.

Angelika's friends noticed a difference in her now that she was in a serious relationship with Vince. "Angelika would date a guy for weeks or months at a time, spending a lot of time in bars listening to music. After she fell for Vince, she grew more domesticated, content to spend her time at home," said her friend Joel Goss.

Vince continued to surprise his friends when he brought up having children with Angelika. "At the age of thirty-four, Angelika is worried that her biological clock is running out. And I'm not getting any younger," he said. Anyone who knew Vince also knew that this meant marriage. His Catholic upbringing wouldn't allow him to upset his mother by having a child out of wedlock.

For Valentine's Day 2014, Vince took Angelika out to dinner at the romantic Shadows on the Hudson. Perched on a forty-foot cliff, the restaurant had a breathtaking view of the lights on the Mid-Hudson Bridge to the north and a never-ending view of the river to the south. After dessert, Vince took Angelika for a stroll on the balcony. It was a cold night, but in every other way it was perfect. The sky was clear, the moonlight sparkled on the water, and Vince made the ultimate romantic gesture. He got down on one knee with a ring in one raised hand. "Will you marry me?"

She looked down at his hopeful face and hers lit up with a smile. "Yes. Yes," she said, wrapping her arms around him. She wanted to hold the ceremony in Latvia on a Baltic Sea beach. She planned to wear a simple dress and go barefoot.

The speed of the engagement was the third surprise for Vincent's friends. Vince's mom, Mary Ann, had a positive first impression of Angelika. On Mother's Day 2014, Angelika shared a photograph of her future mother-in-law seated in a chair with Vince's arms wrapped around her. The caption read: "Happy Mother's Day." Vince commented repeating Angelika's greeting and added: "Your son loves you very, very much."

But others in Vince's orbit were not so sure about Angelika. When they looked at her track record of jumping to one man after another, they began to doubt her love for Vince. They worried that Vince was so smitten with this beautiful younger woman that he could not think clearly. They were afraid that his desire to make up for lost time made him turn a blind eye to Angelika's previous interactions with men.

Friend Sheri Parte told *48 Hours* that she didn't like the violent side that erupted when Angelika was drunk. "She would smack him across the face," she said, while Vince just looked at her without displaying any signs of anger. "Then she'd do it again." Mary Ann confirmed Sheri's story, adding that Angelika once gave him a black eye.

Vince wasn't as bothered by her past—his was littered with failed relationships, too. There was one thing about his new love, though, that Vince did not like—she was a smoker. He persuaded her to switch over to a vaporizer.

However, it soon became clear that Vince was aware of

the trouble brewing in the relationship. Right before Vince traveled with his fiancé to Latvia to meet her family, he sent an email to his sister, Laura, saying: "I hope she doesn't bump me off in Europe." He followed that statement with a funny-face emoji, but the message unsettled Laura. The emotional environment of his and Angelika's relationship was frequently stormy, and Laura knew that truth often lay buried beneath the surface of humor. She was aware of the heat of their fights and, more than once, Vince had told her that he was thinking of kicking Angelika out of his apartment. When the disagreements were resolved and pushed under the rug, nothing ever happened. Laura worried until her brother had safely returned to this country.

In Latvia, Vince walked into Angelika's parent's home for the first time and wrapped her mother in a big hug, saying, "Hi, Mom." While this reaction seemed to contradict Vince's communications with his sister, it served to demonstrate his conflicted thoughts about the situation. According to some of her friends, Angelika and Vince were supposed to get married on that trip, but it didn't happen. Many would later wonder if this could have planted a seed of resentment toward Vince in Angelika's heart.

Angelika had maintained her friendship with Sorluna de Butterfly after her breakup with Mike Colvin, and Sorluna met Vince for the first time at River Station Restaurant in Poughkeepsie in February 2015. She could sense that all was not well in their relationship. Vinny seemed uncomfortable and Angelika seemed distracted and distressed.

Nonetheless, in March the couple vacationed in Manhattan. On Facebook, Vince promised that their next trip would be to visit the Grand Canyon. That was a promise Vince would never be able to keep.

In early April, Vince texted an old friend, Amanda

Hoysradt, about his doubts that the relationship with Angelika was going to last. This was most likely the day that Vince delivered the ultimatum to Angelika: "If you don't get a job by the end of the month, you're out of here. And the wedding is off."

The next day, however, he texted Amanda with a change of heart: "Oh, well, she must be really afraid of losing me because she wants me to stay home and we're gonna make up."

On April 18, Vince and Angelika went to Shadows on the Hudson with a group of friends. Sheri Parte was working the bar that night, but her boyfriend, Monty, joined the party. Outside on the deck by the water, Vince said, "I want to go kayaking tomorrow."

"Are you crazy?" Monty asked him. "Look behind you." Monty pointed to the choppy Hudson. "You can't go out in that water. It's too cold. Don't even think about it."

Angelika had been unusually quiet that evening, barely talking to anyone. Later, when things at Shadows were breaking up, some of their friends wanted to continue the party at a strip club. According to Angelika, Vince wanted to go, too, and have her pick out a girl there for a three-some.

A fight erupted between the couple when Angelika resisted, insisting she was not interested: "If that's what you want to do, fine. But you're going to have to take a cab, because you are too drunk to drive and I'm taking the car to go home."

Their friends talked Angelika into coming along and treated her to one more drink at Schatzi's Pub before calling it a night. At 11:00, Vince and Angelika went home, where they resumed arguing as soon as they walked into the apartment. When they were both tired of raising their voices in anger, they went to bed and made up the way lovers often do.

The next morning, they disagreed on whether to go kayaking and bickered about it for quite a while. Finally, Vince brought it to an end. "We're going. We're going," he said. Angelika acquiesced and threw together supplies while he packed up the Jeep.

Before leaving, Vince texted Laura, informing her that he and Angelika were going kayaking. He described their launch at Plum Point and told her their destination was Bannerman Island. He even sent along a diagram of the locations. He ended by saying he would text her again later that day. The message struck her as off—Vince had never texted her about an afternoon's plans before.

It was the last time she ever heard from her brother. A short time later, Vinny and Angelika headed out on a romantic kayaking trip, and only Angelika lived to tell the tale.

CHAPTER TEN

The day after Vince disappeared in the Hudson River was Marathon Monday in Boston. Sean Von Clauss, who was in New York City that weekend performing four shows, was relieved to be away from his home in Boston, as it bulged with out-of-towners and celebrations before the big event.

Because he was away from home, busy and out of touch with Hudson Valley news, he was unaware of his good friend's tragedy. When he returned to Boston, he had thirty-six messages on his phone—all about the accident in the Hudson River. He listened to every one of them, his shock and horror rising. He didn't want to believe a single word, but the sorrow drowned his resistance to reality.

"My life has forever been changed," he said, "as well as the lives of everyone who knew Vinny. We will never have another cookout or St. Columba gathering. Vinny was the source of peace. He was the peacemaker."

New York State Police detectives continued to pursue information that would explain what had happened on the Hudson River on April 19. In interviews with Vince's friends, they all agreed that the incident made no sense. Many described Vince as safety conscious and insisted he would never have gone kayaking without a life vest. They believed that the presence of only one PFD that day must have been due to Angelika's neglect: either careless or deliberate. They believed that if Vinny had been faced without enough safety gear for both of them, he would have insisted that she wear the vest.

Two days after Vince's disappearance, a small army of family and friends gathered at the river to search the shoreline, with the fervent hope that they'd find Vince injured but still breathing. Laura happened to overhear Angelika speaking to a friend, offering to give away Vince's smoker. She said, "Vinny would want you to have it."

Laura was appalled. For most of them, hope might have a feeble pulse, but it was still alive. Obviously, that was not the case for Angelika, as she was already giving away Vince's possessions.

Vince's lifelong friend Kevin Beisswinger came down to the river to help with the search whenever he could. Angelika's attitude bothered him as well. To him, she appeared to regard the riverbank searches as social events: "She seemed far less shaken than the rest of us."

Nonetheless, Angelika, was present almost every morning to aid in the search. Senior Investigator Moscato was somewhat relieved on the days she did not show up. A missing person case was traumatic enough for those close to the victim, and he dreaded the thought of her being there when they actually found the body. He had given her his cell phone number and they met regularly for updates on the search for Vince. Even on days when he didn't see her, she usually called to check in.

On April 23, the search area was expanded from the area around Newburgh to include Beacon Bridge and Bear

Mountain Bridge. Choppy water kept divers out of the water and bad weather grounded the helicopters, but still they pushed on with shoreline explorations.

That same day, Angelika was interviewed by News 12 Westchester. She wore subdued makeup and barely there lipstick that dimmed her pallor, and a leopard-print top that drained even more color from her face. She had pulled up her hair into a disheveled bun. As she spoke, she alternated between showing her grief—dropping her head in her hands and audibly sobbing—and behaving in a matter-of-fact manner, insisting that she was doing well.

She told the reporter that August 15, 2015, was the planned date of their wedding on the Baltic Sea in Latvia. She revealed more provocative details of the ordeal on the river: "I never wore a life jacket myself when I went kayaking—that was the first time. He insisted that I wear it." She even told the reporter that Vince had told her, "I don't think I'm going to make it," when he was in the water.

When Investigator DeQuarto listened to the interview, he was surprised. DeQuarto had asked her numerous times if Vince had said anything while he struggled, but Angelika had been adamant: the only thing he'd said was, "Call nine-one-one."

The week after Vinny disappeared in the frigid waters of the Hudson River, Kevin Beisswinger wanted to get friends together in Vince's honor at one of his favorite restaurants, Shadows on the Hudson. He worried, however, that it might be too soon, so he reached out to Angelika for her opinion. She loved the idea and immediately took over planning the food, layout, and other details. Kevin was happy to let her run with it—dismissing any misgivings he had by rationalizing that everyone handles grief in a different way.

The group gathered that Friday, five days after Vince

went missing. Many tears were shed as they shared memories of Vince and prayed for the recovery of his body. Angelika, however, was in a far different place—arguing with friends over small details at the event and clearly enjoying the attention.

"It didn't feel right. And each of my close circle of friends that loved Vin from high school began to feel that she was somehow responsible for Vin's 'accident,'" Kevin said. "She was dancing and flirting the night away, as so many of us were grieving and praying that Vin could be found and laid to rest."

Angelika had personally invited Senior Investigator Moscato to the event and said she wanted all the search-and-rescue workers to come to the party. At the restaurant, she had a section roped off with her name on a large sign. On Facebook that evening, she posted a dark, noisy video from the restaurant that drew to a dramatic end as the camera zoomed in on a lonely tea light burning bright on the bar.

Steve Hammond, one of Vince's close friends, was struck by the contrast between the behavior of Vince's ex-wife Suzanne Viafore and his current fiancé. Suzanne was shedding tears and sharing deep, soulful hugs with attendees. Steve could feel the intensity of Suzanne's grief when he wrapped his arms around her. However, his hug with Angelika had a markedly different vibe: "I didn't feel anything, and it just seemed odd. . . . She seemed to be relishing the attention she was getting."

While at Shadows, Angelika called Sean Von Clauss, who was on his way to a music gig at Eleven 11 grille & spirits restaurant in Fishkill, about half an hour from Poughkeepsie on the other side of Wappingers Falls.

"I want to play with you," she said, asking to join him onstage at his performance

"I'm driving. I'll call you right back," Sean responded,

and hung up. He wasn't sure who was calling, thinking it was a different person. When he parked the car, he pressed redial.

Again she said, "I want to play tonight."

Sean thought he recognized the voice but doubted his own ears. "Angelika?"

"Yes, dummy, it's me."

"Are you okay? Do you think Vinny is okay?"

"I don't want to talk about it," she said. "I want to play with you. I want to do 'Hotel California.'" Angelika abruptly disconnected the call.

Angelika left the restaurant, swiping a trifold display card one of Vince's high school friends had created. Arriving at Eleven 11, she requested Sean and his band play "Shama Lama Ding Dong" for Vince. Sean complied, and she slow danced by herself, holding up the trifold and smoking a cigarette.

Then she was ready for "Hotel California," a song filled with dark and ominous lyrics. Her performance was miserable—she forgot the words and stumbled over them, even when Sean prompted her. Following that debacle, she insisted on playing Sean's guitar.

On break, Sean asked her, "How are you doing?"

"I'm happy," she told him.

"What about Vinny?"

Once again, she said, "I don't want to talk about it."

Angelika drank to excess that night and had to get a ride home. Jennifer Colvin, her former boyfriend Mike's sister, came to her rescue.

Vince's friend Jackie Bracco was at Eleven 11 that night, too. "Angelika was a little too happy for someone who just lost her fiancé," she said.

Rumors were beginning to swirl about what had really happened to Vince and how exactly Angelika was involved. Some friends were insistent, in the beginning, that the couple was deeply in love and that Vince would want everyone to give Angelika the benefit of doubt. But because she projected the attitude that a gigantic weight had been lifted off her shoulders, the whispers grew among Vinny's friends. An outlandish theory surfaced that Vinny had declared bankruptcy and was running a scam, faking his death. It was a bizarre theory to embrace, but it was better than the alternative.

The next day, Vince's family came together for mutual solace at Laura and Kevin Rice's home. Angelika was there, too. She smoked cigars, drank scotch, and did cartwheels in the backyard. The family were united in their discomfort—something was not right.

CHAPTER ELEVEN

That same Saturday after Vince's disappearance, miles away from the Rices' home, one hundred people jumped into the water for the Wappingers Creek Water Derby, an eight-mile kayak and canoe race. One group was racing for Vince. "He got us started with kayaking and canoeing," Robin Pierantozzi told the *Poughkeepsie Journal,* "so we can't stop now."

Angelika posted a few photographs on Facebook the next day—pictures of Vince, of her alongside him, and others of some of their friends. She added an unsettling and eerie shot—her smiling face with the Bannerman Castle in the background. Why would she want to celebrate the place, considering what had happened when she'd paddled away from it such a short time ago?

She added fuel to the fires of suspicion on the twenty-sixth, when she shared a photo of the castle from the Bannerman foundation's Facebook page and posted a video in which she performed a cartwheel. She also posted a photo of her doing the same gymnastic stunt along the Hudson

River. Cartwheels had always symbolized celebration, not grief. What was she thinking?

Laura Rice was disturbed by Angelika's behavior and contacted Investigator DeQuarto. "Angelika is acting very strange, unbothered and out of the ordinary," she told him.

Angelika continued to post photos to Facebook of herself and Vince, along with videos of her playing with animals at the Shepherd's View Animal Sanctuary. Finding comfort in the four-legged creatures seemed like a nice sentiment on the surface, but her carefree social media behavior turned unsettling when she also changed her profile picture to a grinning selfie of her making the "hang loose" sign with her thumb and pinkie. The lightheartedness felt peculiar coming from a woman who had just watched as the Hudson River likely claimed the life of her fiancé.

Angelika also took time to call her former father-in-law Richard Graswald Sr. to relay happy birthday wishes to him. He asked her about the accident on the river.

"You know, it's a tragic thing," Angelika replied. "What can I say about it?"

The answer struck him as odd, but he thought no more of it. "My wife and I never had a problem with her," he said.

On April 27, DeQuarto interviewed the three men who'd pulled Angelika from the Hudson River. One described hearing the fire department call about a kayak accident on his scanner. He got into a boat with two others and drove out to the point where they could see Angelika. He said that she was paddling "just fine" toward them and didn't appear to be struggling at all. One of the men said that she was paddling straight for them. When they got within fifty to one hundred feet of her, she seemed to intentionally throw herself into the water. At that same moment, Angelika had lost her connection to the 911 dispatcher. Wearing a life jacket, she was still easy to spot in the turbulent water, but no one on the boat saw any sign of another person or vessel in the water.

The men confirmed that when they pulled her out she was wearing a life jacket and had a black bag strapped over her shoulder. Once on the boat, she'd pulled out an iPhone and attempted to make a phone call. One of them saw the screen light up, showing that the device was working. She'd told them that her boyfriend was missing. They looked around in the water but still did not see another kayak or person in the river. Angelika was cold and shivering, possibly in need of medical attention. They brought her back to shore to get assistance before heading back out to search for two or three hours.

Later that day, Investigator DeQuarto and Senior Investigator Moscato sat down and dissected Vince Viafore's missing person case. Both detectives were baffled by the failure to locate his body. Looking for any holes in their investigation, they realized that no law enforcement had been out to the island. They knew there was a possibility that a body could get hung up on the rocks on that coastline. In addition, there might be something on the island pointing to the mystery of Vince's fate. They couldn't imagine what that might be but knew they needed to search the island to be thorough in their investigation. Moscato made arrangements for a boat to take them on the twenty-ninth.

Investigator DeQuarto asked Angelika to come in for an interview on Monday, April 27. She agreed to stop by the barracks, but she didn't show up. DeQuarto called her the next morning and asked her, "Why didn't you come in yesterday?"

"I was at the animal sanctuary and was having a good time there and just went home after that," she told him. She agreed to come in on the afternoon of April 28.

On the afternoon of the twenty-eigth, Angelika again blew off her meeting with DeQuarto. Again, he called her. Once more, she claimed that she was having too much fun at the animal sanctuary.

"Angelika, you know Vincent is still missing and we haven't located him yet. There's some more information we need to discuss. I would hope this would be your number one priority."

"I'm sorry. I'll come in later."

This time, she did as promised, arriving at the barracks with Laura Rice at 7:30 that night. She sat down at De-Quarto's desk while Laura waited in the lobby.

He said, "I'm sorry to have to get you back in here. I know it's tough talking about it."

"No, I understand, because it happened under suspicious circumstances."

"What do you mean?" the detective asked. It was the first time she'd implied that the incident had been anything but accidental.

"Oh, nothing," she said. "Let's continue."

DeQuarto asked her to go through the events of the day again and to tell him a little about her relationship with Vince. She repeated the same story she had told him the first time. However, she was breathing heavily and soon after they started she asked to smoke a cigarette. The investigator walked her down the hall to a side door and stayed with her while she smoked.

Back inside, Angelika was telling the investigator about her wedding plans when DeQuarto changed the subject. "You lost your cell phone in the water?"

"Yes."

"Well, there's a couple of rescue workers who saw you on your cell phone when you got pulled out of the water."

"Oh, maybe, I don't remember," she backtracked. "You know, somebody has that cell phone."

"Well, Angelika, we need to find that cell phone. That's important."

"You know, somebody has that phone—somebody has it."

"Can you look for it when you go home?" he asked.

"Yeah," Angelika answered, and held her arms tight around her stomach as she breathed heavily again. Once more, she wanted to stop for a cigarette.

DeQuarto continued, "Let's talk about when you and Vincent were in the water. What did he say to you as conversation then?"

"He said, 'Call nine-one-one.'"

"Then you called nine-one-one."

"Yeah."

"Was there anything else said?" he asked.

"No." She clutched her stomach. "I really don't feel good. I think I want to go home."

"Okay." DeQuarto escorted her to the lobby. "Tomorrow, we're going over to Bannerman's Island—me and a few investigators—to do a search of the island and walk the shoreline there."

"Oh great. Maybe I'll see you, because I'm going to the Cornwall Yacht Club to release some flowers in memory of Vinny."

Just before they reached the lobby, Angelika pulled a gift card out of her purse. "This gift card is for you, to thank you for everything."

"I can't accept your gift card. But I appreciate the offer."

Angelika walked up to Laura and announced, "All right. Let's go get some wine and steak."

"I don't feel up to going out to get anything to eat or drink," Laura said.

They exited the building, but suddenly Angelika rushed back in holding a handcrafted figurine, Laura trailing behind. "Here take this, this is for you," Angelika said.

"I can't accept any gifts. But thank you anyway," De-Quarto insisted.

"Are you ready to leave, Angelika?" Laura asked.

"Oh, don't worry about it. I'll just have him bring me home," she said, pointing at the detective.

"I can't bring you home," DeQuarto said.

"Oh, you can't? Why not?"

"Because you have a ride. I just can't bring you home," DeQuarto said. Angelika's flirtatious manner and her attempts at gift giving were very unsettling to him. He didn't know if it was just the way she was or if she was trying to ingratiate herself with him to influence the conduct of the investigation.

With a pout on her face, Angelika followed Laura back to the parking lot. DeQuarto felt relieved as he watched the car drive off a little after 8:00 pm.

Angelika's friend Joel Goss had learned of Vince's fate in a text message from another friend. For days, he heard nothing from Angelika, who was staying at the condo she'd shared with Vince, with a night or two spent at the home of Heather Canavan, the president of Shepherd's View animal Sanctuary.

Then, on the evening of April 28, Joel received a text from Angelika: "Do you have any lemons?"

When he answered that he did, she wrote back: "Come over and bring lemons."

Joel arrived to find Angelika in the kitchen making risotto. While he helped her cook, she focused intently on the task at hand and desperately tried to ignore the reality of Vince's disappearance. One moment, she'd be despondent, exclaiming, "It's been a week!" Minutes later, she would calmly say, "It's only been a week. Maybe everything will be okay."

All night, there was an edginess about Angelika. "She never looked serene," Joel remembered. After midnight, Joel noticed a particularly pained look on Angelika's face and coaxed her outside, where he pulled out his laser pointer with a splinter that caused the beam to form shapes. He made patterns on the leaves of a tree. "They look like fairies, don't they?" he told her.

Angelika was delighted by the distraction. He left the device with her and headed home. Joel was convinced that Angelika could not have been responsible for Vince's death because of her belief in ghosts. "She could not have harmed him because she would fear creating a ghost who would be angry with her from the get-go," he said.

He believed she was grieving, despite the somersaults and karaoke singing, because of his own experience after 9-11. Joel was in New York at the time and witnessed the "many flavors of grief." That was what he saw with Angelika. The only answer for Vince's disappearance, he thought, was that it was a twisted practical joke and Vince would show up in a couple of weeks, laughing at everyone.

The next day, he heard that Angelika had been taken into headquarters by the police.

The cavalier attitude that many thought Angelika displayed in the aftermath of the incident on the Hudson River all caught up with her on April 29. For more than a year, it had been Angelika's habit on Wednesday mornings to go out to Bannerman Island, where she would weed and plant flowers with a group of ten other volunteers.

As she approached the yacht club parking lot that

morning, she again went to Facebook and uploaded a video of her driving. "What a beautiful day!" she exclaimed in the video. Then her phone camera focused on the clock that read 9:22 am. "Nine Twenty-Two is the date that we met," she said.

CHAPTER TWELVE

On the morning of Wednesday, April 29, Investigator De-Quarto received the audio recording of Angelika's 911 call. After what Angelika had told him, he'd expected her to sound exhausted, out of breath, or breathing heavily. But he was surprised to hear nothing to indicate that she had been struggling to come to Vince's rescue.

DeQuarto, Investigator Anthony DaSilva, and Senior Investigator Aniello Moscato, along with two members of the state police scuba crew, Trooper Lance Rell and Zone Sergeant James Whittle, met at Gully's Restaurant on the Newburgh waterfront at around 10:00 am. While preparing the boat for departure, DeQuarto saw he had an incoming call from Angelika. He didn't answer.

Rell and Whittle boarded the state police boat and transported the investigators to Bannerman Island to search the shoreline. Once they'd made it to the island, Moscato received another call from Angelika.

"Where are you and what are you doing?" she asked.

Moscato answered as vaguely as possible, trying to avoid naming his location. Angelika, however, had already heard about their plans from Investigator DeQuarto. She said, "I'm going out to Bannerman's, too."

"Oh, what are you going out to Bannerman's for?"

"To clean up, clear shrubs, and plant more bulbs to beautify the island. And I also have a wreath that I want to put on in Vinny's memory."

"That's very nice," Moscato said. "Maybe we will meet you out there later on."

The detectives walked around the island to get the lay of the land and spotted a few volunteers at work but did not see Angelika. DeQuarto followed the shoreline around the circumference of the island but found no sign of Vince in the rocks and no indication of his presence there ten days earlier.

Just before noon, the three men gathered at the dock and agreed that they'd explored and searched as much as they could without any guidance from Angelika. Moscato called her. She returned the call soon after. "Are you still coming out?" he asked.

"Yeah. I'm on my way out. I'll be there shortly."

"Okay, before we leave, we'll stay and say hello."

Soon the charter boat that transported volunteers back and forth across the Hudson pulled up to the dock. On board with Angelika were the driver, Angelika's friend Katie, and two other women. Angelika stepped ashore, smiling and seeming to be in good spirits. She carried a life preserver decorated with flowers to resemble a wreath. She spotted Senior Investigator Moscato, whom she recognized right away from her meetings with him for the last ten days discussing updates on the search for Vince. She rushed over and embraced him in a warm hug. Moscato introduced her to Investigator DaSilva, whom she had not met before.

She chattered a bit about her responsibilities as a volunteer, then moved away from the detectives to talk to other volunteers and shoot photographs. Thinking her input could add to their understanding of that fatal day, Moscato stepped up to her. "Listen, remember the last couple of days I told you we were gonna need to reconstruct what happened?" he said. "Well, let's concentrate on the time, like the last six hours, from when you left Plum Point and you went kayaking with Vinny out to Bannerman's Island. I want you to tell me, specifically, what you did so that we can figure out exactly, you know, where you parked the kayaks, where you guys went afterwards, in order to give us a better understanding of perhaps where Vinny's body might have floated to."

She led him over to one area of the dock and all three detectives followed. For some reason, she had trouble being definitive about the right spot. "Hmmm, let me think about this. Maybe they were here. Or maybe they were over there," she wavered, pointing in different directions.

To Moscato, she seemed a little bit uneasy. More than once, he had to ask her to focus: "I just need to know what you did. Try to concentrate."

She paced back and forth. She said she needed to have a cigarette. After finishing her smoke, she said she had to use the bathroom. After visiting the port-a-potty, she pointed to the end of the dock that was a bit closer to the island and said, "That's where we parked the kayaks."

The detectives looked at the spot she'd indicated and noticed some guide wires sitting low off the top of the water. Moscato asked, "Are you sure that's where you parked the kayaks, because how did you get under there?"

"Oh, Aniello, don't be silly, you don't know anything about kayaking," she chided. "You don't do it standing up, you do it sitting down."

"You're right, I don't know that much about kayaking.

Where did you guys go after? Did you go up on the island?" he asked, indicating the long flight of stairs leading up to the castle ruins and garden.

"Yeah," she said.

"Can you just walk up the trail so we can kind of create a timeline where you went and whatnot?"

"No problem," she said, but asked to stop at the port-a-potty again before they did.

When she came out, they walked up the stairs to the top of the island and along the trail. She showed them where they had picnicked and pointed out locations where they'd shot photographs. Moscato noticed she had started to clutch at her stomach, breathing heavily as they walked.

"You know, Angelika, whatever you're holding inside you, you have to let out, because it looks like it's burning a hole inside you," he said.

Angelika asked to sit down for a bit on a rock wall that ran along the trail. The investigators joined her.

"Angelika," Investigator DaSilva said, "did you find that cell phone? You told us originally that you lost your cell when your kayak capsized, but a rescue worker saw you with it on the boat. Investigator DeQuarto asked you to look for it."

"Oh yeah, I remember having the cell phone on the rescue boat. I thought I had a missed call. I'll find that cell phone, don't worry. Somebody has that cell phone."

"Where can it be? Let us help you find it."

At this, Angelika's agitation increased. She placed a hand on her chest and her breathing grew deep and loud.

Susan McCardell, another volunteer, was passing by and stopped to ask if Angelika was okay. To Susan, it appeared as if the investigators were bullying Angelika. "Do you want me to stay?" she asked her. "I think I should be here with you."

One of the detectives said, "She doesn't really need you. She's okay."

Angelika confirmed that she was all right and added, "No you shouldn't stay."

Once Susan had moved away from the group, DaSilva pressed Angelika further about the cell phone: "Who did you call from the rescue boat that night?"

"I missed an incoming call and tried to call back, but it didn't go through." Angelika was now pacing back and forth and requested another cigarette.

As soon as her smoke was lit, DaSilva asked, "Where is your phone now?"

"I don't know," she said between inhales. "I had it at the hospital where they took me that night."

DeQuarto chose to jump into the conversation. "Angelika, there's a lot of inconsistencies with what you're saying. I know you're lying to us about the phone, because there's no way you could see it underwater. Then you say you made a phone call with it. Then, that somebody else has it. You have to be truthful with us and let us know what's going on, because we need some closure for the family and for yourself. So, you need to just tell us what exactly is going on."

"Okay," she said finally. "I'm going to tell you everything. I just need a minute."

There was a long pause while Angelika seemed to gather herself.

Finally, she blurted out, "You know, I know no relationship is perfect. We were having problems. Vinny postponed our engagement." She added that he was not treating her right and was forcing her to do things she thought weren't appropriate.

Noting that the conversation was veering toward more intimate personal details, Moscato asked, "Would you just rather speak to one of us privately?"

"Yeah, I'd like to speak with Donnie," she said, indicating Investigator DeQuarto.

The other two investigators headed down the trail while DeQuarto and Angelika sat down on the rocks.

"Just tell me what's going on," DeQuarto began.

"I'm going to tell you everything."

"Okay."

"Can we move to the seating area off the trail, so I can smoke a cigarette?"

"You can go wherever you want," he said.

She led the way to a bench nearby, lit a cigarette, and resumed talking. "You know about the plug, right?"

DeQuarto, who knew nothing about kayaks, bluffed his way past the question: "Sure I do, but why don't you tell me about the plug?"

"What if I did something with the plug?"

"What did you do?"

"I just wanted to be free. I wanted him to be gone. I wanted to be free. I wanted him gone. I wanted to be myself." She blurted the words out quickly, as if she feared she'd lose her courage if she hesitated.

The investigator was stunned by this revelation, and he struggled to keep his face neutral and his focus keen. "What did you do with the plug?"

"I took it out. I removed the plug from the kayak."

"Did you take it out, so his kayak would fill up with water?"

"Yeah," she admitted. "He trapped me."

"Did you take it out on that Sunday?"

"No, I don't think so," she said. "I remember being at the house and taking it out and putting it in a drawer."

"Okay." DeQuarto pressed further. "Well, why did you feel trapped? Why did you feel like you wanted to be free and couldn't be yourself?"

"He always makes these sexual demands to me. He wanted to have threesomes with other women. He demanded sex with me when he wanted sex. He was always wanting to take sexy photos. He expected me to watch pornographic videos with him," she complained. "I felt trapped. I felt I couldn't be myself. It made me want to be free."

"Why didn't you just break up with him?" DeQuarto asked.

"I am a very spiritual person and I knew that he would never really be gone." She paused. "I need another cigarette."

"You don't need to ask," he told her.

Again, Susan McCardell approached them to check in on Angelika. "Are you okay?"

"Yeah, yeah," she said. "I'm fine."

When Susan had left, DeQuarto continued, "Angelika, I know there's more, so tell me what else."

"What else? You know about the paddle? The ring wasn't on the paddle."

"What does the ring do?" DeQuarto asked. "Did you take it off?"

"It holds the paddles together. I think I took it off."

"Did you take it off, so he couldn't use it?"

"Yeah," she said.

"Where is the ring?"

"Somewhere in the back of my car." She pivoted the conversation back to her relationship troubles with Vince. "I just wanted this normal life with Vinny. I wanted to have children with him. I wanted to get married and Vinny didn't want that. He didn't want to get married anymore and that really upset me." She told DeQuarto about one of Vince's coworkers, a woman named Tina, whom she said Vince pressured her about having a threesome with. "Vinny would always say, 'Why can't you do a threesome with Tina—Tina would do this to you and do that.' It upset me."

At that point, Angelika began to ramble and change the subject, but DeQuarto interrupted her stream of consciousness.

"Angelika, let's focus back on what we were talking about. Let's talk about when you were in the water and get back on topic."

"Okay."

"Let's talk about the paddles."

"You know I had his paddle."

"What do you mean you had his paddle?"

"I took his paddle."

"Can you explain to me how you did that?" DeQuarto probed.

"When he was in the water and he was holding on to the kayak and a flotation device, I reached over and took his paddle from him and strapped it onto my kayak."

"Why did you do that?"

"I don't know," Angelika said.

"Did you take his paddle, so he couldn't have it?"

"I guess so."

"Does the paddle float?"

"Yeah."

"So, you took the paddle, so he couldn't have it."

"Yeah."

"Do you think you could have helped him or saved him from drowning?"

"I could have," she admitted.

"But you didn't save him, because you wanted him gone."

"Yes."

"How do you feel about Vinny being dead?"

Angelika shrugged. "I feel fine. I am over it. I feel like I am myself. I feel free." She sounded almost bored.

"Because of what you did, you caused Vinny to drown."

"I guess I did."

DeQuarto needed to hear a definitive answer. "Angelika, I need the truth. Did you intentionally remove that plug from the kayak, so he would drown?"

For a moment, she stared down at the ground, not saying a word. Finally, she raised her head and said, "I guess I did."

"Does anyone else know what we talked about up here?"

"No. Only my diary."

"Okay. Is Vinny in the river?"

"Yeah, he's in there." She looked out at the water. "Hopefully, he'll come up soon."

DeQuarto knew it was time to reunite with his colleagues and fill them in on what he'd learned. "We'll go back to the barracks and we'll sit in a more formal environment," he told Angelika. "We'll discuss what we talked about up here in some more further detail."

"No problem. I feel better telling you about this because you feel like a real and caring person," she said.

She and DeQuarto walked back over toward the other investigators. While she paid another visit to the port-a-potty, DeQuarto joined the others.

"You're not going to believe this," he said, "but she just admitted to killing him. She said she pulled the plug."

"A plug? What do you mean a plug?" Moscato asked.

"Yeah, I didn't know about it either, but apparently there's a plug in the . . . [kayak] and she pulled it out."

"You gotta be kidding me."

"No."

"She told you this?"

"Yeah. She also said the paddle has some kind of ring on it that she manipulated or took out so that the paddle would collapse."

"Are you *kidding* me?" Moscato said again, clearly shocked.

"No."

"She said all this? Where's she going now?"

"Oh, she's going to the bathroom."

"Okay," Moscato said. "Maybe we should keep an eye on her."

When Angelika emerged from the facilities, she spoke to her friend Katie, who asked if she was okay. "I am," Angelika said, indicating the investigators. "I'm just going to be coming with them for a bit."

At that point, putting Angelika in handcuffs would have been a by-the-book move. However, since they were riding a boat, there was the possibility that a problem could occur, and the last thing investigators wanted was for the woman in custody to drown because she was restrained.

The uncuffed Angelika climbed willingly onto the state police boat. On the ride back, her anxiety seemed to have dissipated and her mood lifted. She threw a flower in the water in memory of Vince. She leaned into the wind and whistled a tune. "I'm free!" she shouted.

Shortly after departure, the boat engine start sputtering. The scuba crew brought the boat to a halt in the middle of the river. They pulled out their tools and soon had the repairs done well enough to get them to the opposite shore. As they waited, Moscato held onto Angelika.

"What's the matter," she asked, "you think I'm going to jump off?"

"No," Moscato said. "It's just that I'm not that good of a swimmer myself."

"Don't worry," she told him. "I will save you."

Twenty-five minutes after they'd left Bannerman Island, they were back at Gully's. Senior Investigator Moscato rode alone in his own vehicle. Angelika sat in the front passenger seat of Investigator DeQuarto's car, with Detec-

tive DaSilva in the back seat. On the ride from the waterfront to state police headquarters, Angelika talked about
how much better she felt after their conversation on the
island. At the end of the fifteen-minute drive, she spotted
a motorcycle in the parking lot and said she wanted to get
on one and go riding. Then she turned to Detective De-
Quarto and said, "I thought you were cute since the first
time I met you."

The investigator was completely taken aback. He mut-
tered a thank-you and entered the barracks with Angelika.

CHAPTER THIRTEEN

At 3:20 that afternoon. Investigator DeQuarto swung the interview room door inward and Angelika stepped into a joyless, confining little space with no windows, scuffed white walls, boring gray carpet, a utilitarian table, and three padded but uncomfortable-looking chairs. Angelika was wearing a floor-length patterned skirt and a tank-top blouse, holding a bottle of water in one hand and a pair of white sandals in the other. DeQuarto followed after her, still in his jeans and T-shirt.

She sat in the chair next to the side wall, beside the end of the table. DeQuarto took a chair at the opposite end, sitting perpendicular to Angelika. Their interaction began with a bit of idle chatter about yoga and going to the gym. A cold Angelika swung her legs up and down, rubbed her hands together, and blew hot breath on her fingers to warm herself in the chilly air-conditioned room.

DeQuarto pulled out a card and read Angelika her Miranda Rights: "'You have the right to remain silent. Anything you say can and will be used against you in a court of law. You have a right to have a lawyer present while you're being questioned. If you cannot afford to hire a lawyer, one will be appointed to represent you free of charge before any questioning if you wish. You can decide any time to exercise these rights and not answer any questions or make any statements.' Do you understand that?"

"I do," Angelika said with a nod.

"You understand all these rights I explained to you?"

"Yes."

"We had a very good discussion," he said.

"We did."

"I think you felt better."

"Yes."

"I know you probably don't want to run through this again, all right, but it's just what we need to do."

Angelika nodded again.

Unsure if her edginess had more to do with the cold or nerves, he tried to get her to relax. "This will be like therapy for you."

"Of course," Angelika said.

"Like I said, you'll feel better."

"You will, too," Angelika said with a smile.

"Okay. I will. And you're right. I definitely will," DeQuarto agreed.

"Can I get a little close?" Angelika asked.

"Sure," DeQuarto said. Angelika scooted her chair up toward him until their knees were about two feet apart.

"Let's start with your relationship with Vince," the investigator began.

"Hmm-mmm," she mumbled, wrapping one arm around her waist.

"So how long were you guys together?"

"A year and seven months."

"How did you meet?" DeQuarto asked, leaning forward on the corner of the table with one arm, the other resting on his thigh.

She told him about meeting Vince at Mahoney's Irish Pub.

"Were you guys living together right away or not?"

"Pretty much, yeah." When he asked for details, she estimated the date she'd moved in with Vince and gave the address of their condo.

"From your point of view, how did you think your relationship was? Describe it to me."

"Just like any couple, we had our issues," she said.

"What issues would that be?"

"Um, miscommunication." Pressed to elaborate, Angelika said, "He pushed for everything. He pushed for sex—sexual stuff."

"Okay, he always wanted sex?"

"Yeah."

"And you do sexual things?"

"Well, yeah."

"Okay."

"He wanted threesomes, porn, everything."

"Okay."

"I just was not ready. In time, I might give it all to you, but I can't right now."

"Did he ever force himself on you?"

"Yeah."

"He does?"

"Yeah." But then she immediately contradicted herself. "There was no abuse."

"No?"

"Mentally, it was rough," she admitted.

"Okay. And why was it rough?"

"Because he pushed—he pushed."

"And you mean by pushing—you mean what you just described?"

"Yeah, like special stuff. He demanded it every day, he

wanted to do it on the weekend," she said, brushing a strand of hair away from her face and behind her ear.

"And you just plain were not ready?"

"No."

"And you let him know that?"

"Mmm-hmm," Angelika acknowledged. "That's why we fought."

"You fought a lot about that?"

"Mmm-hmm."

"What did he say about it?"

"He said I should want it."

"Did these fights actually get worse as the relationship went on?"

Angelika said that he gave her a couple of slaps, grabbed her, and pushed her, but she claimed that she never hit him. They discussed the stress she felt from Vince's sexual demand and how, although she made sure he knew about it, she tried not to express it in a negative manner. Part of her way of coping was to write it all in her diary.

The investigator grabbed on to that tidbit. "Do you keep your diaries?"

"Yeah, they're in Russian."

"They're in Russian? Do you keep those in your house—your apartment?"

"Yeah."

"Did he ever see them—he didn't know Russian?"

"He was studying Russian, actually," Angelika said.

"Oh yeah?"

"Yeah, we wanted our kids to speak Russian."

DeQuarto shifted back to the sexual conflicts and her anger over it. "What were you thinking inside as this was going on?" he asked her.

She sighed and cleared her throat before answering. She told him it made her feel ridiculous, rubbing her hands with increasing speed across the skirt covering her thighs. "I want to be with him and I love him, but he's not letting me be myself."

"The way you want to be without any restrictions or anything like that?"

"Yeah."

"Now, together, as far as [him] holding you back, does it mean you couldn't be certain things, you couldn't talk to certain people?" DeQuarto clarified.

"Yeah, and wear this, and don't do that."

"Did that make you angry as well?"

"Yeah. I wanted to be away from him."

"Away from him?"

"At times. I've written more," she said, referring to her diary.

"So why didn't you just break up with him?" DeQuarto asked.

"'Cause I loved him," Angelika said. "I wanted to make it work. I wanted a kid. I wanted a family." Angelika said, echoing the sentiment in singer Amy LaVere's lyric: "Killing him didn't make the love go away."

DeQuarto played along, saying that he could see that she loved Vince a lot.

"I don't think he loved me," she said suddenly. "He always doubted me."

"Did he? How did he doubt you?"

"He'd accuse me of cheating. He'd accuse me of lying. Lying and cheating."

"A lot?"

"Not a lot. We had our great moments in our relationship." But she continued to tell DeQuarto about Vince always being suspicious and picking on her.

DeQuarto brought up Tina, Vince's female coworker, probing for the signs of jealousy Angelika had hinted at on the island. Now, though, she insisted that Vince and

Tina were just good friends. She claimed she got along with Tina but had expressed irritation to Vince for his always talking about her.

The investigator then moved to questions about their last night together: the parties at Shadows on the Hudson and Schatzi's Pub and the fight that followed. "What were your thoughts that night?" he asked.

"Scattered," she said, clutching her stomach and swinging her legs back and forth.

When the questions turned to that fatal Sunday morning, she started rubbing her hands together vigorously. She told DeQuarto that Vincent had insisted on going kayaking, despite her objections about the roughness of the river.

When she got into the car, Angelika said, "I had my life vest. I had my purse. Vinny didn't take his life vest."

After briefly revisiting their activities on the island, DeQuarto directed her to the trip back.

Angelika said that when they left the island on their kayaks, Vince was next to her, but then he pulled about fifteen feet ahead. "The way he was paddling was not good. I said, 'No. You have to do it like this,'" she told DeQuarto, and slouched, rounding her back and resting her forearms on her thighs to imitate the proper posture.

She continued, "We were just piloting, dealing with the wind and the waves, the current, the turbulence [as] the tide was changing. So he went to the right of me for a little bit, showing off, and he kept riding the waves vertically and that's wrong because the kayak is small and very long."

"Okay," the investigator said with a nod. "I know what you mean."

"And he was going on the wave and I'm like, 'No, you've gotta turn it and you gotta ride *in* the waves.' He said, 'Okay. That's right. Watch me! Watch me!' I said, 'You're not doing it right.' We were joking and he pulled . . . [in front] of me and said, 'Baby, this is the adventure of a lifetime.'" Angelika paused. "I didn't feel like that—that was when I started to realize that this was serious. I knew he had no cap on the kayak."

"The cap? You mean the plug?"

"Yeah, the plug. I'm sorry," Angelika clarified.

"Where does the plug go on the kayak?" De Quarto asked.

"It's all the way in the back."

"Underneath it?"

"No."

"No? Why don't you draw it for me?" The investigator slid a piece of paper in front of her.

Angelika sketched while she talked. "See, the kayak is long and there's a dry compartment over here."

"Is the dry compartment in the back?"

"Yes. The beer was in there—the beer and the water."

"Where does the plug go on the kayak?" DeQuarto asked, still finding it hard to believe that the plug was not on the bottom of the vessel.

"It goes all the way to the back and it drains it."

"Like underneath it?"

"No. It's like when you're putting it on a car, you pick up your kayak, drain it."

"Okay." DeQuarto decided to move on. "So, he didn't have that plug in there? Why didn't he have that plug in there?"

"He didn't have it because I guess I had it."

"You took it out of the kayak at one point?"

"Uh, yeah."

"When did you take it out of the kayak? That's what we've got to get to, you know," he told her.

Angelika cleared her throat and pulled her knees in closer to her chest. "The kayaks were in the living room in winter—all winter, they were in there." She added that the couple's kitten had chewed on the plug and Angelika had removed it to stop her from destroying it, putting the plug in a desk drawer in the office area of their home.

"Okay. When did you take that plug out? That's what we have to get to. We need all that information. We've got a piece we've got to figure out, okay? As long as you're being honest—"

Angelika interrupted. "I am being honest. I'm trying to remember."

"Absolutely," DeQuarto backtracked. "But we have to piece all these pieces together. We have to know if that's an important part—"

"Very," Angelika interjected.

"So, when did you remove . . . [the plug] from that kayak? Did you remove it at your house?" he asked, looking for a definitive date.

"It was either at the house or in his car."

"That Sunday," DeQuarto said, leaning forward again with a forearm resting on the corner of the table, "did you remove it from the house or from the car?"

Angelika rested her chin on the palm of her hand to think. "No. It was before—way before."

The investigator kept pushing for specifics, and Angelika kept giving foggy answers. She said that if Vince's kayak had been taking in any water on the way to the island or when they tried to go around the island to the beach she didn't notice it and Vince didn't mention it.

"But you knew that plug wasn't in there?"

"From Plum Point, yes."

"From Plum Point, you knew it wasn't in there?"

"We were already in the water and I said, 'Yeah, where's your plug? Are you kidding me?' I was mad at him."

DeQuarto asked her to go back to the moment of the accident.

"He was in the water . . . the waves were doing their thing," she said, making rough undulating movements with her arm, "up and down like that, and he's going in and out of my vision. And then I saw that [the kayak] started to fill up and I knew that plug wasn't there. I kept paddling and paddling and trying to get closer to him, but I couldn't."

The investigator asked whether the kayak flipped or sunk, but Angelika said she wasn't certain because her vision had been partially blocked by the turbulence in the water. She said it was possible a wave had flipped him. She'd seen him in the river holding on to his kayak, his dry bag, and the seat floatation cushion.

Angelika sighed and sniffled deeply, becoming choked up. DeQuarto placed a hand on her forearm and gently said, "It's all right. It's all right."

After a moment, she continued, "And his paddle—I can't remember if he handed to me or if I just pulled it."

"Why would he hand it to you if he needed to get back?"

"Well, he wouldn't need it at that point," she said, explaining that it was not possible for him to right his kayak in the water.

"Did he hand it, or did you take it?"

"He handed it," she said, motioning outward with her arm. "And I took." She pulled her arm back toward her.

He reminded her that she'd previously said that the paddle was floating and asked her to focus.

She sighed again, her shoulders raising and lowering. "I guess I took it."

"You took it from him?"

"'Cause he was already losing it and it was floating over," Angelika explained.

"And what did you do with it?"

"I put it on the side of my boat."

"And then what did you do?"

She sketched the positioning of the boat and told DeQuarto how difficult it had been to secure the paddle, since it was missing a piece and coming apart.

"When you say it was missing a piece, what do you mean?"

Angelika sighed, as if frustrated with the investigator's ignorance of kayak equipment. She picked up the pen to illustrate but stopped before drawing anything. "I knew it was missing a piece—a part."

"When you say missing a part, what do you mean?" DeQuarto asked again.

After another exasperated sigh, she said, "The paddle that he had—every paddle—comes apart and there's a little connector ring for security. He didn't have that ring."

"Why didn't he have that ring?"

She blew out a forceful breath and leaned back in her chair. "He loaded the frigging paddle and he didn't take it."

"What happened to that ring, then?"

"I think it's still in the truck," Angelika mused.

"Who took the ring off of there?"

"I did," she said, clasping her hands together and resting her forehead against them. She spent a moment collecting herself and then said, "He's the guy who loaded and unloaded the truck."

But then Angelika contradicted herself, saying that she didn't take the ring off. DeQuarto pressed her on it, and after a long pause she said that if the ring was in the back of the truck then Vince had removed it.

"Did there come a time when you took that ring off at home?" he asked.

She said that she remembered seeing it in the car and that the paddle could be used without it, but it's not as safe. "He's in the water," she remembered. "I have both paddles and I get—I keep—and the waves keep pulling me away from him, further and further. That's when he yelled, 'Call 'nine-one-one.'"

DeQuarto, remembering the inconsistency with this

statement and what she'd told the News 12 reporter, prompted, "Did he say anything else to you?"

"No," she said firmly. She then told him about her efforts to reach Vince but how, despite all her paddling, the distance between them kept increasing. "I watched him bobbing up and down in the waves."

She described the call to 911, that she'd known she was rambling but couldn't stop, and the operator's repeated commands to stay on the line. She told DeQuarto that Vince always worried about her safety, was very protective of her, and always made sure she had everything she needed.

"When you say he was always protective of you, how did that make you feel?" the investigator asked.

"Limited," Angelika said.

"Limited?"

Rubbing her hands together again, she said, "Yeah, caged."

"Like you wanted to break free."

"I just wanted to be myself."

"Okay. And how could you accomplish being yourself?"

"How? Letting go?"

"Letting go of your relationship? Letting go of Vinny?" DeQuarto pressed. "Did there come a point in your life, particularly on [that] Sunday, when you realized it was the opportunity for you to let go?"

Angelika admitted that, in a spiritual sense, something had felt off about their return from the island, but she'd set it aside, believing that Barbara—the Bannerman volunteer coordinator—and her husband were watching them from up on the hill and that all would be well.

"When you went to Bannerman's Island that day, did it cross your mind that you would be leaving there alone?"

"Not on the island."

"When you were in the water?"

"When I saw that his boat was starting to sink in the water," she said, lowering an outstretched hand increment by increment.

"Why did you think his boat was sinking into the water?"

"Because the plug had been taken out."

"Did you feel relief when you saw him going into the water?"

"No. I was frustrated with him because he rushed me. He always pushed me and rushed me. 'Go, go, do this,' and I'm like, 'Just give me a minute.'" She added that she felt a bit like that right now.

DeQuarto explained that it was important that they know everything right now. Angelika had raised up on her knees from her cross-legged position and readjusted her body. When she settled back in the chair, she sat back on her heels in a slouched hero yoga pose.

Angelika continued to be vague as DeQuarto tried to nail down a confession. When the investigator asked her why she had removed the plug, she explained she'd wanted to use it to make a cat toy. But earlier, she'd told him she had taken it off so that the cat wouldn't play with it.

"No. No. No," DeQuarto said. "You're going off on a tangent. Let's stay on track here. On the way over here in my car, you said you felt better. I want you to feel that way again, okay?"

"I will. We all will," she said.

"And what's the only way to get to that point?"

"The truth."

"Exactly," the investigator agreed, leaning forward.

"The truth is," she said, turning away from DeQuarto and grabbing her stomach, "I wanted to have kids and to be married and live happily ever after. He told me he wanted the same thing."

She continued listing the problems this had caused and then said, "He said he couldn't take it anymore."

"Couldn't take what?" DeQuarto asked.

"Me."

"Did he tell you that?"

"Yeah."

"Do you feel free now—free now that he is gone?"

"Yeah."

"You feel that you can do everything you want now?"

"Um-hmm."

"Do you feel happy now?

"Um-hmm."

"That's understandable 'cause you're you, right? You have to be you," DeQuarto said, trying to keep her focused. "What did you guys discuss on the island, though? Did you discuss any of this before the incident?"

Angelika shook her head. "Not this. We concentrated on taking pictures, selfies."

"When we talked before, I asked you, I said, 'Do you think you contributed to the drowning?' Do you remember that?"

Angelika said she did.

"Do you think it had anything to do with that plug you'd taken out?"

"Well, obviously," she acknowledged.

"What about the oar—uh, the paddle?"

After saying initially that she'd taken the ring off, Angelika now changed her story, stating that Vince had removed it.

DeQuarto pressed for a more definitive answer on when and where she'd last seen the ring, but Angelika insisted she was trying to remember. He told her being honest now would be in her interest, since "everything is going to surface, sooner or later—whatever transpired in your relationship and that night."

She kept insisting she was trying.

"I'm not going to judge you for what you tell me—I'm not going to think of you differently for anything you tell me in this room," DeQuarto said. "The only way we are going to get around this and over it—close it—is to lay all the details out. It's got to be the truth, Angelika, everything that happened, so I can piece it all together. Otherwise, we're never going to close it. I want that, and I want you to know I think you are a great girl and I think you need to know. Am I right when I say that?"

"Not necessarily. A little bit."

"A little bit? That's what I'm here for, to give you support. But I need you to give me the truth—reciprocating this, okay?"

His next few questions didn't make much progress with Angelika. Then he asked, "How did you know the ring wasn't on the paddle that Sunday?"

"Because I saw it somewhere."

"On Sunday you saw it?"

"No. Before that. I saw it in the apartment on the floor." After more prodding from the investigator, she said that she'd also seen it in the back of the Jeep that Sunday. She insisted that the paddle hadn't concerned her, since it could function even without the ring. She claimed, however, that she was concerned about the missing plug. She littered this information with more rambling about the psychological nature of her relationship with Vince and a premonition she'd had as they left the island that he wouldn't make it back, calling his accident "destiny."

DeQuarto made another plea for her to open up and tell the truth to help the investigation. "Vincent's gone—not mentally, not emotionally, but physically. That's it. And there are people who need closure with this. You need to just open up with me, okay?"

Angelika hung her head and sniffled. The investigator

scooted his chair a bit closer and patted her knee, hoping to comfort her. She turned her head away to the far corner of the room and used both palms to wipe her face of tears. "Talk to me," DeQuarto encouraged. "Everything that's inside of you—let it out. I'm telling you, you'll feel so much better than you are once you do it. That weight— that knot that's in your shoulders now? That will be gone."

Angelika continued to talk about the love she and Vince had shared and made a strange remark: "He wanted to go," she said.

DeQuarto dragged her back to the core question. "You know exactly what took place and that's what I'm trying to get to. This girl felt like a trapped person—"

"I had a lot of anger issues," Angelika interjected.

"She was forced to do things that she did not want to do, and that's why this took place. I can't explain you saying, 'He wanted to go. . . .' How did you want to get rid of him? What did you do to do that? I know how much it can build up inside you. I know how the anger can explode. Am I right when I say that?"

"Yeah, of course."

"I need to know what happened that led to him drowning. That's what I need to know. That will put closure to this whole thing and a lot of people will be able to move on from this. So, I need you to explain that to me."

After a long pause, Angelika said, "The bottom line is I just wanted to be free."

"How did you obtain that? How did you make that happen?"

"By being myself."

"How did being yourself bring you to this point?" De-Quarto pressed.

"I'm drifting," she said, putting the heel of her hand against her forehead.

"Don't drift. This is the hurdle we need to get over, right here at this point. Once we get over this—"

Again, Angelika slid into another side issue and the investigator brought her back to the point.

"We're talking about him drowning—drowning in the Hudson River. You know what happened that day. You," he said, pointing an index finger at her. "We're eventually going to know what happened, after this whole thing is said and done. I wanted to hear it from you, exactly what happened so I can help you. If I find out through our investigation—which we will—I can't help you. You need to tell me, you need to be honest with me, about everything that happened in that river and what led up to him drowning."

Angelika was silent for a while, sighing and resting her forehead on the palm of her hand from time to time. "I don't know what to say."

"I don't expect it to be easy—I really don't. But I do expect that you want to tell me the truth."

"Yes."

"And you want to help yourself, at this point. And that's why I'm here for you."

DeQuarto leaned forward, his posture a mirror image of Angelika's. So close, their knees were nearly touching. But although he kept his eyes on her face, she turned hers away, staring at the floor or the wall. "I'm going to be honest with you," he said. "You know I'm an honest person. I've been talking to you all day. What happened out there I don't believe was an accident. It wasn't an accident. All right? I don't believe that at all. There's a lot of people who believe this. I know there is more to this story. You've got to tell me the story. There's no clear-cut way around it."

"It's a big, long, drawn-out story, there's a lot to it."

"[What] I am trying to focus on is that it wasn't any

accident. It was destiny, or it was supposed to happen, you say. Okay?"

"The circumstances. Everything."

"The circumstances that caused him to drown. That is what I need for closure, what you need for closure."

"You need me to take the blame," Angelika said, staring at the wall.

"It's not that, Angelika. It's not that. Believe me. This is turning into something where people need to move on, okay?"

Still, Angelika insisted she needed more time.

The investigator urged her not to think about it, just let it all out. "You know what happened that night. You need to tell me. You need to be honest with me. It needs to be the truth."

After a protracted pause, Angelika said, "It's hard to say."

DeQuarto acknowledged she was right but said, "Tell me exactly what happened in that river."

Finally, Angelika said, "What led up to his drowning was me, my actions letting him go."

"Like what? You letting him go in front of you is not going to cause him to drown. He sunk in his kayak, right?"

"Yes."

"That was not accidental. I don't care how you look at it, it wasn't accidental. Did you take that plug out to get yourself free?"

"Could be."

"Is it 'could be' or is it 'yes'?" DeQuarto urged.

"I'm just trying to understand myself. Like how and why did I do that?" she said, as if to herself.

"Do you maybe take that plug out because it was an escape for you to set yourself free?"

"Yeah, but I didn't want to kill him," Angelika insisted.

"Did you want to be free?"

"Yeah, but I still wanted to have kids with him."

The investigator reiterated his certainty that it was not an accident and exuded empathy for the love she and Vince had shared, her mixed emotions, and her perception that Vince had been preventing her from being herself—all in an effort to get her to confess. "You had mixed emotions—you wanted him to drown, but you wanted him to stay living. Yes or no?" DeQuarto asked.

"Yeah."

"I want to know what he did to lead up to this night to make you want him to go. It almost feels like this was an outburst in reaction to the way he treated you. That's what I think. Am I right when I say that?"

She agreed.

"It was almost a way to get back at him for the way he treated you?"

"Kind of."

"You said, 'I'll take the plug out. I'll take the ring off—'"

"I didn't take the ring off," Angelika said.

Although disappointed she was contradicting what she told him earlier that day, he let it go and moved to another topic: "When you watched him in the water, was a part of you saying, 'My worries are goin' away now, and I'm free'?"

"Yeah."

"And you were almost . . ."

"Euphoric?" Angelika volunteered.

"Euphoric that he was gonna be gone?"

"I was just—I was . . ."

"You felt that way?" DeQuarto prompted.

"Yes," Angelika said. "I still do."

The investigator acted unfazed by that concession, but he had to have felt an icy chill creep up his spine when she acknowledged the sociopathic part of her nature. "Did you feel that the only way to get away from him was to—was his drowning?"

"That night, when I saw him already there in the water," she said, spreading her arms out wide. "I guess that's true."

"Do you think deep down inside of you, if you really wanted to, that you could have saved him?"

She nodded her head.

"Did part of you decide not to because you want to be euphoric and free? Is it correct that you wanted him to drown because of all this stuff that built up over time?"

"That's correct."

"Do you think you could have saved him by holding on to the oar—or paddle?"

"I couldn't—"

"When you took the paddle from him—"

"I didn't take it. He pushed it. It floated to me and I took it."

At the one-hour mark, DeQuarto rose to leave the room. Angelika pushed up on the arms of her chair and unfolded her legs, commenting on the pins and needles and requesting a bathroom break. The investigator knocked on the door. When it opened, he walked out of the room, followed by Angelika.

CHAPTER FOURTEEN

When they returned from the restroom break, Angelika said, "The truth is: he didn't really love me. And I was ready to let it go."

But when DeQuarto asked if she had something else to tell him about what happened that night, Angelika clammed up again and told the investigator she was hungry. He left again to order a pizza.

Alone in the investigation room, Angelika stretched her legs straight out from the chair and rotated her ankles before bringing her feet down to the floor and swinging them back and forth. When DeQuarto returned, Angelika suggested that she had a lot of stories she could tell him. He reminded her of the focus of the session: a missing person who was probably on the bottom of the Hudson River. He brought the conversation back to the matter at hand: "I asked you when we talked about Bannerman's: what actions did you think contributed? And do you remember what you told me?"

"It could be me," Angelika recalled.

"Then I asked you why could it be you? What did you do?"

"I wanted to be free," she said, wrapping an arm around her midsection.

"You wanted to be free, but I said, what did you do *physically* that caused him to drown? And let's see if you remember what you told me."

She pleaded an inability to remember, and he offered to refresh her memory. "You said, by taking the plug out of the kayak and taking the ring off the oar or the paddle. Does that sound correct?"

She wouldn't quite admit to her previous statement, but she admitted that things had sort of come together. DeQuarto suggested that the accident was a perfect opportunity and she agreed.

"Am I going to find anything else when I do a search of your house?" the investigator asked.

"Well, we had guns—"

"No. I mean anything else pertaining to this incident."

"The ring will be in the house—in the car or in the house."

"What are your diaries going to say when our Russian interpreter reads them?"

"You're going to read all my thoughts and how I was unhappy."

"Did you talk about his death at all?"

"No. I might have mentioned that I just want to get away. I never wrote anything that said I want to kill him or anything like that."

DeQuarto circled back around to the location of her cell phone. She rambled on, talking with her hands and demonstrating moves she'd made as if she was trying to mentally re-create the night and her phone's role in it. Eventually, the investigator told her not to worry about it, that they would get the complete records from her cell carrier.

She said there was one more thing he needed to know: Vince was mad at her for stopping her birth control. "To be honest with you, I think I had a miscarriage."

"Just now?" DeQuarto asked, stunned.

"I'm sure of it."

"Do you need an ambulance?"

She said, "No."

"Are you sure?" he insisted.

She assured him she was fine and there was nothing to cause any worry or concern.

Taken aback by her laissez-faire attitude, he continued and asked why she'd had the car keys that day.

She explained that both of them always carried a set of keys.

"You brought both sets with you on the kayaks?"

"Yes."

"Why?"

"Because I didn't trust him. He was not always focused. He has a memory thing or something."

DeQuarto then asked a series of questions about Vince's life insurance policy and why she was on it when they were not married. She explained she needed proof that they were in a domestic partnership to enable Vince to put her on his employer's health insurance.

The discussion then returned to the tumultuous relationship between Angelika and Vince. "Was he at all irrational?" DeQuarto asked.

"Sometimes."

"Like how?"

"He was not giving me air, ever. He was constantly suffocating me. He would not leave my side. He would not let me go to the store. He would not let me be for a fucking second. Even when he was at work, he'd come home and say, oh, Peanut said this and that."

"Bringing up other girls?"

"Yeah, bringing up other women all the time and putting me down. I'd bring it up and he'd say, 'I'm not putting you down.'" She went on to repeat her claim that Vince was always pushing her for sex. She said that when he insisted and she complied it dredged up the memory of when she was raped years earlier. She'd once told him, 'Whatever you want from me, just take it.' "He did take it forcefully, more than once," she told DeQuarto

The investigator wore his empathy like a badge of honor. He wanted her to feel as if he were on her side, that he believed all her complaints about Vince, while all the time hoping he would break down her resistance and give up the kernel of truth buried between the layers of rationalization and denial. "As much as he made you happy, he made you unhappy."

"It was fifty-fifty."

The investigator tried to get more from her, but she said that she had told him everything he needed to know. "At this point, I'm over it. You know, I'm not that kind of person. I am over the rape. I am over the forceful stuff. I will never—"

"Are you over Vinny?" DeQuarto interrupted. "You can just go on?"

"Yeah."

"That makes sense. Now you'll never have to experience it again." DeQuarto rose from his seat. "Just hang out here for a minute. I'll be back. Don't go anywhere."

"Would you bring me my purse? I need to get a tampon." Once she was alone, Angelika slipped on her shoes, sipped water, and wiped her underarms with tissue. She stood and walked to the two-way glass, where she flipped her long, waist-length hair to settle behind her back, flicked at spots on her shirt, and did a couple of yoga stretches. Then she sat back down at the table and fiddled with her necklace.

After a minute, apparently unable to stay still, she pushed down on the arms of the chair, raised herself up, and folded her legs underneath her body. She then fooled around with her hair, pulling it back, holding it up, and combing it with her fingers. She sat hunched over, folding and unfolding a tissue in her lap.

When DeQuarto returned he didn't have her purse but told her someone had gone to the store for tampons.

They talked again about phones: the one she had in her purse now and the one she said she'd dropped in the water, which she insisted were two different phones. She said that the bag she'd taken out in the kayak was at home, but it was still wet. DeQuarto asked if the phone could still be in there.

DeQuarto returned to the moment she was pulled out of the water by rescuers. "Did you know he was gone?"

"I couldn't see . . . it was dark."

When he probed her about when Vince had actually drowned, she insisted that she tried not to think about it. "I know you try not to think about it," he said, "but it is something we haven't discussed."

Angelika nodded her head. "Umm-hmm, I was safe, and I knew he was gone. . . . I admit I was glad."

The investigator tried again to nail her down on removing the ring from the paddle. Again, she said it was either in the Jeep or on the floor of the apartment. She told him that she and Vince had talked about the missing ring. She'd suggested to him that they shouldn't go kayaking that day because of its absence, but he'd brushed off her concerns.

DeQuarto again walked her through their departure from the island in the kayaks. For the first time, she said that while Vince was still in his kayak he'd said, "I don't think I'm going to make it."

DeQuarto was surprised at the difference in this

statement and pressed her for details. "He was still in the kayak."

"Yes."

"When he yelled to you, 'I don't think I'm going to make it,' did you call nine-one-one then?"

"No. I called nine-one-one when he told me to."

"Was he still in the kayak?"

"No. He was in the water." She added that he'd had one arm over the kayak and another over the paddle. He held the floatation device and the bag with the camera in his hands.

"Now, did you really want to save him?" he asked.

Angelika gave a big, long sigh and said, "Yeah, somehow. If he did not say call nine-one-one, I would have fucking paddled the shit out of myself and got to him somehow."

"That's a little different than what you told me earlier, though," DeQuarto said. "Why? Why do you keep changing what you're saying? You're confusing me."

"I'm tired," Angelika complained.

"I know you're tired and that's a real issue for me. You say one thing and then you go to another. I feel like you're not telling me some things—"

"About the night, right? Not overall."

"Why do I have this feeling that you're not telling me the truth?"

"I'm not lying to you. I'm not," Angelika insisted.

Angelika said that she felt a lot of guilt and DeQuarto wanted to know why.

"Why? Because I didn't want anyone hurt. I never wanted anybody hurt."

"So why do you feel guilt?"

"Because of the thoughts I had. I wanted to be free. I wanted him to drown."

"That's understandable. Do you feel guilty for other things that happened that night?"

Angelika gave a long, rambling response, and DeQuarto cut her off: "You watched him drown. It's difficult. I know—"

"I didn't just watch him drown," Angelika said, her voice sparked with anger. "I tried to do something about it."

After a few more questions, DeQuarto left the room. Angelika fiddled with her bracelet, drank water, and did yoga stretches in her chair. Then she stood, rearranged the water bottles on the table, checked out her face and hair in the two-way glass, and did a few standing stretches. Her boredom filled the room like a dark cloud.

When DeQuarto returned, he wasn't alone. Investigator Matt Skarkas, in a light tan suit, entered the room with him. He introduced himself to Angelika and pulled up another chair at the corner of the table.

DeQuarto asked that she tell her story again, starting at Plum Point. Angelika laid it all out again with Skarkas occasionally interrupting her to get clarification, covering many of the same points already visited by the other investigator.

After a short while, DeQuarto walked out and Skarkas continued the questioning alone. Skarkas tried, without success, to pin Angelika down about the time between when Vince went into the water and she called 911 and the amount of time that elapsed between when she last saw him and when she was pulled from the water.

"Ultimately what this is about for me, and for Don, [is] to sort of understand what you were feeling and how he made you feel that made you do what you did and take out that plug and know that he was going to drown in that river. Okay? So, let's go through that."

"Okay," Angelika reluctantly agreed.

How did he make you feel? Why did he have to be dead at that point?"

"Because he made me mad."

"In what way?"

"In a lot of ways."

"Well, what did he specifically do to you?"

"He never hurt me physically," she said. She spoke about the happiness in her relationship and how one day it would be here, the next day totally gone. "He was constantly talking to me—'you gotta do this, you gotta do that. I won't marry you until then.'"

"Did it upset you that he sort of switched that he did not wanna marry you?"

"Yeah, of course," Angelika replied, indignant. "Who proposes to somebody and then changes their mind?"

"Did he give you a reason why he changed his mind?"

"Yeah."

"And what did he say?"

"He wanted me to open up."

"What did he want you to open up to about?"

"Everything."

Skarkas asked for details and she described his controlling behavior—how he wanted to know where she was and make sure she locked the door when she left the house.

When Skarkas said that it all sounded like safety issues, she said, "I felt safe with him, but I felt better when he was not at home."

Skarkas continued to push her for precise answers about her feelings. She said that she never wrote about how she wanted to kill him, but she did write that she'd simply had enough.

"How long ago did you get to that point that you had enough, and you wanted him gone?" he asked.

She paused for a long while and then said that she

couldn't give an exact time. Getting nowhere, Skarkas asked if she had ever thought about killing him in another way and why she decided on the drowning. Getting no real response, he tried again: "When did you decide that your life would be better without Vinny in it—with Vinny gone? When you made some of these choices and decisions that you knew, ultimately, was going to lead to this?"

Angelika still wouldn't answer directly but said that she did nothing to stop his drowning from happening because a part of her wanted him gone. She admitted that after she was rescued her overwhelming emotion was relief that he was gone. She wouldn't admit that she overturned her kayak to make the people on the rescue boat think she'd done everything she could for Vinny, insisting she'd done it to "experience the water."

Switching tacks, Skarkas turned the questioning to the cell phone she'd had on the island. She said that the one she had with her was an old one and she had no idea where the new one was. She could only assume that someone who was there that night had it, but there were a lot of people on the shore. She added that she'd taken her old phone to the AT&T store and had it reactivated the next day. The account was in Vince's name. "I called Laura the other day and she freaked out because it showed his name," she said.

"If you had to tell his family why he had to die, what would you tell them?"

"Laura and I will have our own closure eventually," Angelika said cryptically. "I don't know. You can't tell them he was a bad person or anything like that. I can't."

"What would you tell me—if you had to tell me?"

"That's different. I can tell you."

"What would you tell me? Did he do anything to you, sexually or some other way?"

Angelika didn't respond.

"Listen," Skarkas continued, "to feel strongly enough that you feel an overwhelming sense of happiness that a person dies, there has to be some real reasons beyond that someone is a little controlling. I want to understand exactly what led you to make those kinds of decisions. What were some of the things he made you do?"

Angelika sat still in her chair with her head bowed. When she moved, she shook one hand as if trying to remove some unseen contaminant. Then she rested her elbows on the table with her forehead in her hands. "I don't have any specific examples of things."

"Look. When you want someone dead, there are reasons why that made you feel so strongly in such a way to feel that sense of happiness that he's in the water and he's going to die. And that's what we're here for, to try and understand that. What did he do?"

"He pushed me," Angelika said vaguely.

"Specifically, what did he do?"

"He wanted me to be fully his, sexually. He wanted to own me."

"Is . . . [this] something you noticed about him when you were first together or did it start coming out—"

"It started coming out a month or two in the relationship," she said.

"Did you ever talk to him about that?"

"Yeah. We had daily conversations."

"How did that make you feel?"

"Trapped. Trapped."

"So, as he starts taking in water, do you get that sense of happiness, of relief that he's going to be gone?"

"Yeah."

She then told Skarkas that it had been a very happy day on the island until the very end, when she'd grown angry at Vince because he was rushing her to leave. She insisted that she didn't think about him not making it back until his kayak started taking on water.

As Skarkas continued to pepper her with questions about the paddle and the ring, Angelika grew exasperated: "You guys know what you know, so yeah, for fun, I took the oar."

Skarkas assured her he wasn't putting words in her mouth and left to get her a cigarette. Angelika paced and went into a yoga pose.

After a couple of minutes, DeQuarto walked in with pizza. She told him she'd rather have a cigarette. He assured her they would get her one, but for now she should "just sit down and relax."

She didn't sit but took bites of pizza as she paced heel to toe across the length of the room. DeQuarto returned with a cigarette, matches, and an ashtray and then left her alone to enjoy her smoke. She lit up and then sat cross-legged on the floor against the wall.

When Skarkas returned to the room, Angelika remained on the floor, smoking. He asked if she'd put anything into Vinny's beer, which she denied.

"At this point, we know what happened, we're just trying to get an understanding of it. So it's better to talk about this openly so we get all the facts, you know what I mean?" Skarkas said.

Rather than answering, Angelika questioned whether or not the sprinklers would go off since she was smoking a cigarette.

After discussing the plug once again without garnering any new details, the investigator asked her about her diaries and where they were. She told them she'd been keeping them since she was thirteen years old. The older journals were at her parents' house and the current ones were on top of the desk or in a drawer. She said that she wrote in them when she was happy and when she was depressed, but she hadn't written in them at all since Vinny died.

When asked who she had been in contact with since the accident, she said, "Nobody."

"No one?" Skarkas said.

"Except you guys."

"What two guys?" Skarkas asked, misunderstanding what she had said.

"Just you guys," she repeated.

"Oh, 'you guys'—meaning us, the police," Skarkas said. "That's it. You're only talking to the police for ten days?"

"Yeah. And my family and friends."

"Well, that's what I'm talking about. Who are the friends and family you were in contact with?"

Angelika became defensive, swearing she didn't talk to anyone about what happened. Finally, she answered as vaguely as possible, "The whole world, man. Everybody." Then she insisted again that she didn't share any of the details because "no one . . . [could] handle it."

Once again, she asserted that all Vinny had said to her was "call nine-one-one." She was too far away from him to hear anything else.

"I sense that you wanted him dead," Skarkas said, "but you also didn't want to do something that was up close and personal. Was it easier for you to be far from him and not really be that close to him when he was in the water?"

"I found it easier, but I tried to get closer."

"But you wouldn't save him, one way or the other."

"I could have," Angelika said.

"I know you could have, but you wouldn't," Skarkas said, "because you obviously wanted him to be gone, you wanted to be free, correct, yeah?"

"Yeah."

Skarkas moved back to the paddle and Angelika stated firmly, "I did not take the ring off."

"It seems like you're waffling on that, back and forth."

"Well, I'm still trying to remember."

"But you knew it wasn't there."

"Well, I knew it. I saw it. When I took the paddle from him, I looked at it."

Skarkas asked her for details about the ways Vince had pressured her about sex. "Okay, being tied up, what else?"

"To just be available to him at all times."

"Are there going to be toys in the apartment?"

"Oh yeah. He had a sex bag."

"What kind of things are going to be in that sex bag?"

"Well, uh, handcuffs, blinds," she said, motioning an eye covering across her face.

"Did you allow him to use some of those things on you?"

"No. I don't like pain. I told him that and he was fine with that."

"What are some of the things he would have liked to have done that would cause pain that you wouldn't do?"

"He wanted me to be strapped to another girl and I refused." She added that there were rings in the bedroom for fastening the straps.

The investigator asked if she ever participated in those type of things in another relationship and she said she had not. "So, this was a foreign concept to you?" he asked.

She admitted that she'd thought about it, indicating that she believed everyone did. She said that when Vince had done things to her she'd felt ashamed.

"To the point that you wanted him dead?" Skarkas said, throwing his arms wide as if saying, "Ta-da."

Angelika, however, did not answer.

Skarkas continued to probe: "Did you feel like this was your only way out?"

After a pause, she said, "Yeah, I guess so."

But when asked if she feared what Vince might do if she tried to leave, she said, "He was civil. He was very civil. He was a good guy in that sense."

While Angelika smoked a second cigarette, Skarkas went out to find her a cup of coffee. Using the pack of matches, she tidied up the area in front of her, scraping pizza crumbs and ashes into the ashtray. For a while, she sat very still with her head hanging low. She transitioned briefly into seated yoga stretches before returning to her previous static pose. Her lack of emotion was chilling.

CHAPTER FIFTEEN

DeQuarto and Skarkas returned to the room, DeQuarto carrying Angelika's purse, and DeQuarto asked if he could have the keys to the Jeep. She told him to go ahead and get them out. DeQuarto didn't want to go into her bag to retrieve them, but Angelika insisted. They left after a couple of minutes, with DeQuarto promising to get the fan turned on to pull the smoke out of the room. Skarkas returned moments later with coffee and excused Angelika to go to the restroom with a female officer.

When Skarkas and Angelika had settled back in with cups of coffee, Skarkas continued his push for a confession. "This is your window of opportunity," he said. "This is for you to provide what I call your slice of the pie, your version of the truth from your perspective. There's only one person in the world that can provide that perspective, and that's you. You don't want other people or other things to portray a picture of you that's going to be unfair. And, obviously, the facts are what the facts are. We obviously talked about some of them at length. And one of the things I want to tell you is that we're the police, we're not the morality police, you know what I mean? And I know that you said, 'Oh, this is fucked up,' or whatever, but you know what? What's more, this is real life. This is real life. I know that they say everyone walks around with their pro-verbial masks on or whatever, but that's not really what goes on behind closed doors, people's relationships and lives and there's explanations for everything. One of the things I wanted to talk about is some of the time frames we talked about just don't match up."

"Okay. Which ones?"

"From the time you leave Bannerman Island to the time you make the nine-one-one call, all right? That duration of time is about forty minutes, which is right around—is long enough for you to be back at Plum Point, you know, onshore."

"Yeah."

When he pointed to the delay before she called 911, she elaborated on her story. Originally, she'd told him that all Vince had said was, "Call nine-one-one." Now she claimed she'd asked, "Right now? Now when I'm trying to save you?" and he'd repeated his request to call 911.

Skarkas challenged her, encouraging her to be honest. "The fact of the matter is, you didn't want to save him. We talked about that. You don't have to sugarcoat it. Listen, you wanted him gone, right? Did you do anything to make that happen more quickly? Did you pull the oar away? Did you pull the kayak away?"

"No. I didn't pull the kayak or oar away," she said, shaking her head.

Referring to the kayak paddle, Skarkas said, "You said to me before that you took it. In taking that oar, it was a part of you that wanted him to be gone. You knew taking that oar from him—"

"I didn't take it from him on purpose," Angelika in-sisted, suppressed anger strangling each word. "I didn't take it from him, like grabbing it from his hand so he couldn't have it." She paused, trying to organize her words before speaking out loud.

She told Skarkas that she could see Vinny's kayak filling up with water because of the missing plug and the forceful waves. "He handed me the oar."

"Why would he do that?"

"And I took it," she said. Adding more detail to the conversation while Vince was in the water, she now said that she had urged Vince to swim toward her.

"My question to you, and I'll be direct, you wanted him to be dead. You took steps for him to die. Did you do anything at that moment that made it easier, faster or better? You know what I mean. You didn't want to save him. You wanted to be free. You're trapped. You're in this relationship that you feel trapped in, that you wanted to escape from."

Angelika didn't deny his assessment but said, "All I did was try to paddle towards him and stay afloat myself and make sure the phone was in my lap, just in case I needed to call."

"The thing is when he goes under—and we've already talked about this—there was a sense of happiness and relief which, regardless of what anyone else may think, those are your emotions, those are your words, your feelings, not mine. Okay?"

"Okay."

"Like I said, we've got to own our words, own our feelings. You wanted him to be dead. He goes under the water. You know he's going to drown. There's happiness and some relief. Did you do anything to make sure that was going to happen? Did you do anything to make sure you can feel that relief? Did you take the oar out of his hands? Did you pull the kayak away from him?"

"No. None of that."

"You just didn't do anything proactively to try to save him."

"I did," Angelika insisted. "I tried to paddle towards him. But my arms were tired."

"Why did you do that if you wanted him dead?"

"I didn't. I didn't and I did."

Skarkas kept trying to prompt her into a direct answer. "At that moment, did you do anything—besides the fact of obviously taking the plug out—did you do anything beyond that to make sure that was going to happen?"

"I stayed on the line with nine-one-one. What I should have done was make the call and then paddled, but I didn't."

Then he asked about the witness who'd observed her intentionally capsizing her kayak. "Why did you do that? What's the real reason why you did that? What did you want them to think?"

"That I was trying to save him."

"Okay."

"That I was doing everything I could to save him."

Skarkas asked if she'd had her story planned out before she left Plum Point. Angelika denied it, shaking her head vigorously.

Investigator Skarkas asked her to describe her whole day again, leading up to when she and Vince drove to Plum Point. As she told her story, Don DeQuarto returned to the room and slipped back into his seat against the wall.

Angelika repeated her claim that she did not think about the possibility of Vince dying in the river that day until his kayak started taking on water, DeQuarto reminded her that she'd told him she wanted Vince to have a good final meal and that when they'd stopped at Wendy's she'd considered that his "last supper." That, he said, showed that she was thinking about it before arriving at the riverside.

"I don't want to talk about my past," she said. She rose and walked over to the door, her back to the detectives.

Skarkas said, "You don't need to talk about your past."

She walked back to the table, wiped tears from her eyes, and returned to her chair. DeQuarto encouraged her to release whatever she was holding back. She said that she couldn't say it—she could write it in her journal, but she could not speak of it.

"Tell us what was going through your head that afternoon about what was going to happen on that Hudson River," Skarkas said.

She struggled to find words, making senseless hand gestures as she worked up to a full sentence. "It just felt like something good was coming out of it."

"Out of his death? Something good?" Skarkas asked.

"I had to go along with the traffic that day."

"That makes sense," DeQuarto said, "but can you explain it a little more, so I can get a better picture?"

"I'm very stubborn," she told them, steepling her hands. "And I'm set in my ways. And go for what I want. And no matter how long it takes, I get what I want, regardless of others. I keep on moving forward. I help people who are necessary for what I want."

"What do you want?" DeQuarto asked.

"I want to travel the world—"

"No, what did you want that day?"

"That day? I wanted to be free," Angelika said.

"And you wanted him to die."

"If you put it that way."

"I'm not putting it that way. What's the answer? You know what the answer is. What's the answer, Angelika?"

After a pause, she said, "I wanted him gone."

"And that would set you free."

"I didn't want him, like, *gone,* gone. That's why I wanted to have a kid."

"You wanted him gone, but he would live on in the child. His spirit would live on," DeQuarto said, appealing to her strong sense of spirituality.

Angelika nodded her head and mumbled an unintelligible response.

Skarkas moved the discussion to the moment Vince had capsized: "What are your feelings and emotions knowing that this was going to happen?"

"I'm like, ripping in two halves," Angelika said. "You know, like angels and demons."

"Mmm-hmm. What's the demon side saying?"

"The demon side—ah, it's not a good side. You guys don't want to see that side of me."

"Nobody does," Skarkas said.

"That side was telling me: This is what's going to happen, just let it happen. Just let it—but the good side was saying: Save him. Save him. You can do it. You're strong."

"Why did the demon side win out?" DeQuarto asked.

"Well, because of the way he was treating me, you know."

"We've all got that. One little guy has a pitchfork, the other has little wings, right? Sitting on our shoulders. Sometimes one wins, sometimes the other."

"I'm reckless, reckless. I have no fear."

"Did you realize the devil side was coming out?"

"Yeah, yeah, like when it gets dark outside."

"That's what I asked you before," Skarkas said, "and maybe now you'll open up. The demon side, did you do anything else when he was in the water that would ensure that he would die out there? Did you take that paddle out of his hands? Did you pull that kayak away? Did you do anything?"

"I did not pull that kayak. I did not pull the paddle."

"You just knew that you didn't need to do anything, that he was going to drown?"

"Yeah, yeah." She told them her "two sides" hadn't argued about what to do.

Skarkas disagreed. "You know, I think there was some of that. You said you knew he was going to die. You knew it was his last day. There was this happiness and relief when he goes under the water. When you took that plug out, that was the first step. That was the demon side of you knowing that was the first step towards making you free?"

"I don't know. I don't want to think that, but I guess so."

"I know you don't want to quote, unquote, *admit* it, but it's the truth. Correct?"

When Angelika did not respond, DeQuarto said, "So you're free."

"Yeah."

"You got what you want."

After Angelika let out a heavy sigh, Skarkas said, "When we're done, you can cover it back up again, that's fine. But for now, how long before that day were you thinking about a way he could die, and you would be free?"

"I wasn't," she protested, throwing a hand over her mouth.

"Really?" Skarkas said, his voice dripping with sarcasm.

"The way to be free. We were planning a wedding on August 15, which is exactly fifteen years since I came to the states—that was a day that was meaningful to me."

"But that's not what I'm asking," Skarkas said. "What I'm asking you is when did you think, 'He needs to die and I'm going to take some steps to make sure that happens'?"

"'And be free,'" DeQuarto added.

"'Be free. And be out of this controlling relationship.'"

"I wasn't thinking that," she said.

Angelika wavered as Skarkas asked the question again and again. She balled her hands into fists in her lap. Once they were on the island, she said, "I had my towel in my hand and I said I'm unhappy and I'm going to end it."

"Then you were what? Your emotion?"

"Happy."

DeQuarto asked, "Did you think those thoughts when you guys had an argument the last time?"

"That was Saturday night."

"You wanted to be free?"

"I always wanted to be free."

Skarkas pressured her about when she took the plug out, insisting it was that Sunday, but Angelika stuck to her original story that it had been a while since she had done so. Skarkas wasn't buying it. "No way, no way," he said. They argued, Skarkas getting progressively more belligerent. When Angelika had had enough, she asked to speak to "Donnie" alone. Skarkas granted her request and left the room.

"I did not take the plug out that weekend," she told DeQuarto. She asked him if he wanted the date she'd removed it.

"I just want the truth," he said.

Angelika pleaded for more time to think. She breathed deeply. Her legs tucked underneath her body, she extended her hands across her thighs and made yoga mudras with her hands as if in meditation practice.

DeQuarto played the good cop to the max. He talked about being with her from day one, learning about her, and coming to understand her. "You let me in today. Yes, and you know what? That made me understand why this happened—everything, why this incident took place. It made me understand it. And you know what was before that?"

"What? A great big jumbled mess."

"It looked like—it didn't look good. But now it's explainable why something like this happened, because I know what happened in your past. And it was okay to tell me that because it made me—it painted a picture for me of what occurred. Like I said. There's a little piece you're still holding back from me. I'm not here to hurt you. I'm not. I'm here to help you through this. To help everyone through this. To put this to bed. To close it." He pushed her to tell him why she took the plug out, but she steadfastly said she did not know why.

She seemed as if she wanted to answer his questions but couldn't. No matter how many ways he posed the question, she said that she couldn't remember when she'd removed the plug and the ring.

"I know you took that plug out the beginning of April, but I want to know the reason why you took it out. I know why. You know why. We both know why, but I need you to—"

Angelika finished his sentence. "To set it free."

"I need to know the reasoning why you took that plug out. I need you to be straight up with me. Honesty. The truth will set you free." He then moved to talking about what she did to cause Vinny to submerge in the water. She said she hadn't done anything and DeQuarto reminded her that was not what she'd said earlier.

"Well, you keep asking me," she said in an exasperated tone.

"That's because you keep changing your story."

"Because I don't remember the whole thing," she argued.

"Put yourself in my shoes—"

"I know everyone thinks I'm lying and I'm on drugs and I'm not—"

"I don't think—listen, I don't think you're on drugs—I'm not judging you at all."

"I know *you* are not. I'm saying out there."

"We're trying to complete an investigation here. Do you know how much hours and time we put into this?"

"I'm sorry."

'No, you don't have to be sorry. We've spent a lot of time—helicopters, boats—there are a lot of unanswered questions that are going to surface and a lot of them are going to surface with time. We've put in so much time and caring for you not to give me one hundred percent."

"I'm doing that—I'm trying to."

He acknowledged that she was having trouble remembering and that was okay, that it was why he was spending so much time with her. She admitted that she wanted Vince gone and their kayaking trip was an opportunity for that, that she knew the kayak plug was out that Sunday, that there was a possibility that the kayak would fill up with water, and that he drowned as a result. She also admitted again that she felt better now that he was gone and she was free.

They ran through the timeline again. Then DeQuarto left her in the room by herself.

She swung her legs restlessly and then tried to sit still and focus on her breathing. Soon she was up doing yoga stretches to settle her nerves. She had just started a series of warrior poses when Skarkas returned to the room. She continued her yoga as he asked her questions. First, he wanted to know how she'd met DeQuarto at the island that morning and she said she'd called him. He confirmed that she went there of her own free will. Then he asked about the memorial at Shadows and she said it was for his friends.

All the while, Angelika continued doing yoga and Skarkas had finally had enough. He asked her to take a seat. She said she didn't want to.

"I'd rather you sit, please."

For a while she just stared at him, then took a few deep breaths and returned to the chair. Her mannerisms turned drastically different. With DeQuarto, she'd relaxed in a slouch in the chair and kept her eyes focused on him when he spoke. Now with Skarkas, her back was rigid and she looked at the wall, the floor, or the surface of the table.

Where DeQuarto was beseeching and sympathetic, Skarkas was blunt. He told her she was lying and he told her she'd killed Vince. She countered that she wasn't lying but also didn't want to admit to killing him.

"The truth is, you took that plug out because you wanted to kill him, you wanted him to be dead, you wanted to be free."

Angelika argued again that she'd taken the plug out a long time before.

"Because you wanted him to die," Skarkas pointed out.

"Yes," Angelika said.

"We're talking semantics. By taking that plug out, you killed Vinny. Correct?"

"Correct."

"And you wanted that to happen. Correct?"

Angelika took a breath and arched her back. "Correct."

"And you feel happy and relieved that it happened, that he's dead."

"Yes."

After a twenty-second pause, Skarkas said, "See, that wasn't all that hard."

"No," she said. Still not looking at Skarkas—still maintaining a firmly erect spine. She said that she had to go home and take care of her cat and asked to finish the discussion later.

"Angelika, the reality is this, okay?"

"Go ahead."

"You killed Vinny. Right?"

"You're telling me."

"No, I am asking the question and I want to you to tell me the truth."

"I am telling you the truth."

"What is the answer to the question?"

"I didn't want him—"

Skarkas cut her off, "Angelika, what is the true answer to that question?"

"All right. I'll give you the fucking statement."

"What is it?"

"I wanted him dead and now he's gone. And I'm okay with it. I'm okay with it."

"That's not good enough."

"I want to do my yoga and I need to pee again from that fucking coffee."

"Angelika, here's the thing: when somebody is dead, there's a certain amount of accountability we all have to take."

"Okay."

"Okay. And you obviously have a level of accountability that you have to take."

"Yes," she said. "Am I going to jail?"

"Yes. I'd say it's a pretty good possibility, yes."

She nodded.

"I'm thinking you knew that, right, when you came here?"

"No. What about my cat?"

"We'll take care of your cat, I promise you that. Is there someone you want us to call to come get that cat, that you feel comfortable caring for it?"

After some protesting, Angelika gave him a few names and Skarkas left the room to find someone to take her to the bathroom. As soon as he departed, Angelika eased into a casual slouch, as if a huge burden had been lifted from her shoulders. Moments later, Skarkas popped open the door to let her know that her cat had already been taken care of by Laura—he had food and water and was doing fine.

Every minute must have felt like eternity as she sat in that bland room with no object to take her mind off her current state of affairs. How could she keep her mind focused? How worried was she about going to jail that night? What did she expect? The abyss of the unknown stretched in front of her and the investigators made it clear that she only had herself to blame.

When Skarkas returned, he asked again about the location of the cell phone she'd lost. She again said she did not know where it was and denied that she had destroyed it.

Skarkas then asked a series of questions that would become a key point of contention with the defense team. "Your journals, what were they written in?"

"Russian, but some in English."

"But obviously, you're well versed in reading and writing in English."

"My native language is Russian."

"But you can read and write in the English language, correct?"

"Yes, of course."

Skarkas asked if she wanted coffee and she expressed a desire for tea. A few minutes later, a female in uniform walked in with a tray and served it to her.

The investigator asked a few more questions and then told her that they had background and paperwork to do and he would check with her later. Again, as soon as he left the room Angelika's posture relaxed.

After sipping some tea, she got to her feet and practiced yoga breathing and some basic poses. On occasion, her poses lapsed into awkward stillness, as if the reality of her situation was interfering with her ability to maintain her focus on yoga.

Skarkas came back with more questions about some belongings in the apartment she'd shared with Vince. He wanted to know where to find the keys for the lock boxes, her diaries, and any weapons. Angelika provided what information she could and the investigator started to leave the room.

"May I ask you a question?" she asked.

"Yeah."

"Miranda warning. What is Miranda? Who is Miranda?"

"That's what Donnie read you—"

"I know. who is Miranda? Why that name?"

"That was named after a case."

"Which case?"

"The People versus Miranda."

"A case?"

"A court case."

"Who versus Miranda?"

"The People."

"So, a person is named Miranda. Who was Miranda?"

"That was a person who got arrested."

"I want to know the story."

"You're going to have to look it up."

"Give me my phone," she said with a grin.

Skarkas laughed and exited. When he returned, Angelika was sitting cross-legged on the floor. She remained there, seeming more relaxed in his presence that she had been previously. He questioned her further about Vince's life insurance policy. She stuck by her original story: that it was Vince's idea and she had no idea about the amount of money involved.

As soon as the investigator departed, she recommenced her yoga practice, incorporating *ujjayi* breathing and more challenging poses than earlier. She appeared to achieve a higher level of focus this time around. When she came to the end of her routine, she relaxed in Savasana, or corpse pose. Then, after a swig of water, she kneeled by the table and rested her head on her folded arms.

By midnight, she'd been in the room alone for more than an hour and a half. A few minutes after midnight, Investigator DeQuarto entered the room to see if she needed anything. All she wanted, she said, was to go outside. DeQuarto said he'd ask his boss for her.

Forty minutes later, as she was still alone and sitting at the table, the boredom had to have been driving her batty. Shortly after 1:00 am, she reread the Miranda warning, set it down, and started playing hopscotch. Finally, a female officer led her out of the room for a much-needed change of scenery. When she returned to the room, just after 2:00, she sat down in the far corner where nothing but a fraction of her arm and skirt were visible to the security camera, as if she just realized the position of the device and how to avoid it.

Finally, DeQuarto and Skarkas entered the room with a third man, a Russian interpreter. "Angelika, we found someone from your home country," DeQuarto said. He introduced the man and asked her if she wanted to sit up at the table, but she declined.

"We just have a couple of quick things. In the house, Vinny had guns, right?" DeQuarto asked.

"Yes."

"Do you know, technically, what kind of guns they were?"

"No."

"Okay. Because there's one gun that's missing. There are magazines for it and bullets for it, but the gun's not there. Do you know where that one gun might be? Have you seen all of his guns?"

"No."

"No?"

"I don't know how many he had, maybe four."

"The fourth one's not there."

"I remember seeing the rifle. I remember seeing one handgun. I think he had another."

"And that's it?"

"Yeah."

DeQuarto moved on. "As far as your diary here, I've taken a bit of a look. Pretty interesting stuff. But at the end of it, does it just end, or is there another continuation page or another diary that continues from this one?"

"On this last page here, obviously I can decipher this. . . ."

The Russian interpreter stepped in and spoke to her in Russian, reading from the last page. After they had conversed for a while, Skarkas stepped in. "Angelika, where's the plug?"

"It's in the drawer," she whined.

"That's for the oar."

"The ring was in the drawer then?" she asked.

"Yep. Where's the plug?"

Angelika could not—or would not—give an answer. Skarkas kept pressing. "If we put divers in the water over there, are we going to find it?"

She then insisted that it was in the car but could not say where. As the questioning continued, DeQuarto left the room.

"Obviously," Skarkas said, "if we find it in the water, you've just destroyed your credibility with that. I don't care if you tell us, 'Yeah I took it out before we left the island.' That makes sense. 'I tossed it in the river,' that's great. Whatever. But it was taken out before that, you said, so it's either in the car or in your apartment."

"Yes."

"So, if we have to send someone back there to look for it, where is the most likely place to find it?"

"In the car."

"Where would it be in the car? In the trunk? In the seat? In the glove box?"

Angelika mentioned a couple of possibilities and added, "Obviously, I don't remember." She added that since she had a little kitten, it could have been knocked around anywhere.

"You think about it and let me know," Skarkas said, and left the room. The interpreter followed him out.

At 2:30 am, a female guard walked in and asked Angelika to stand. When she did, the guard led her out of the interview room.

The eleven-hour ordeal was over. A new one was about to begin.

CHAPTER SIXTEEN

On Monday, after Angelika Graswald had spent eleven hours in an interrogation room, Investigator DeQuarto filed a felony complaint against her stating that she had committed second-degree murder, intentionally causing the death of Vince Viafore.

The document, however, contained no indication of how she'd accomplished this act of second-degree murder.

Later that day, Major Patrick Regan, the Troop F Commander of the New York State Police, stood before reporters at the state police barracks in Middletown and read a statement: "'The New York State Police at Montgomery and the Orange County District Attorney's Office announce the arrest of Angelika Graswald, age thirty-five, of Poughkeepsie, New York, for murder in the second degree, a Class A-one felony.

"'On Sunday evening, April 19, 2015, state police responded to a report of a missing kayaker on the Hudson River. At approximately seven forty pm, Angelika Graswald contacted Orange County nine-one-one and reported that she and her fiancé, Vincent Viafore, both of Poughkeepsie, New York, were kayaking on the Hudson in between Plum Point and Bannerman Island. Graswald reported to nine-one-one that Viafore's kayak capsized due to choppy waters and she could not locate him in the river.

"On Wednesday, April 29, 2015, State Police Investigators who had been pursuing leads in this case obtained enough information to charge Graswald with intentionally causing the death of Viafore.

"The investigation into the circumstances surrounding the murder remains ongoing. Anyone with information is requested to contact the New York State Police. . . .

"Graswald was arraigned in the Town of New Windsor Court under the Honorable Richard W. Thorpe and remanded to Orange County Jail without bail.

"The body of Vincent Viafore is yet to be located and efforts to locate him remain ongoing. The New York State Police are seeking the assistance of the boaters, hikers, and fishermen on both sides of the Hudson in locating Mr. Viafore's body and preserving the discovery area for any possible forensic evidence that may exist. If anybody encounters anything that they believe might be connected to this incident, they are asked to call the New York State Police before disturbing anything in the area of the find.

"In efforts to pinpoint or reconstruct the last hours, minutes, and seconds of Mr. Viafore's life, the investigators have maintained contact with Ms. Graswald. Initially, we believed her to be a survivor of a tragic accident. [While] . . . trying to piece together the best places to locate him in the river and what may have led to what occurred, some inconsistencies of the accounts she gave of those last minutes led investigators to be suspicious."

When a reporter asked about the inconsistencies, Major Regan responded, "She implicated herself in her involvement in his intentional death." He added that they believed Vince had been killed in the water, not on the island. "We believe we know what happened. We believe she indicated how this occurred."

In the immediate aftermath of the charges being filed against Angelika, her friends refused to believe that she could possibly have done anything to harm Vince. Some of his friends found it difficult to accept, too. "I do not want to believe she murdered my friend," Sean Von Clauss told *People* magazine. Amanda Bopp, who'd known Vince since before he started dating Angelika, said, "She made him so happy. I know he was so in love with her. I'm not passing judgement on Angelika at all yet. I don't know what to think." She added that she found it impossible to believe that the petite woman could have overpowered Vince.

After her arrest and incarceration at the Orange County Jail in Goshen, Angelika, like all inmates, was screened for placement and suicidal ideation. Although she was not deemed at risk of taking her own life by standard assessment procedures, the transporting officer reported that he thought she might be, because she was acting in a strange, "almost cheerful manner" for someone who had experienced a significant loss. She was placed under "constant supervision" because of his input and "due to the severity of her crime."

After her arrest, Angelika gave a series of interviews to local and national media. She insisted to Blaise Gomez of News 12 Westchester that she had been falsely accused of intentionally causing Vince's death. The reason, she believed, was the diary entries she had written about Vince's interest in rough sex and threesomes. She'd also written that she wished he were dead. She claimed those statements were made in anger during a problematic patch in their relationship. She asserted that she was very much in love with Vince—they loved each other, problems and all. She told *People* magazine that she felt the police had tricked her into telling them what they wanted to hear. With regards to her suspicious behavior in the immediate aftermath, she told WNBC New York, "Of course I didn't do it. He was the love of my life. It was a crazy time. I was doing crazy things."

An attorney with the Legal Aid Society of Orange County prepared for Angelika's preliminary hearing, scheduled for May 5 before Judge Richard W. Thorpe in the Town of New Windsor. But the hearing was canceled because the grand jury was still in session working on the case.

Soon after her incarceration, Angelika was sent into lockdown for yelling an expletive at a female corrections officer and adding, "I will spit in your face." This was the first of four incidents requiring disciplinary action in her first few weeks behind bars.

May 8 was a consequential day for Angelika. The Embassy of the Republic of Latvia in Washington, D.C., entered the fray, with a fax requesting to be informed about any court dates and their outcomes. Even more pivotal was the arrival of Richard Portale as Angelika's new defense attorney. Portale had short brown hair, prominent cheekbones, and an engaging smile—when he chose to use it.

Portale came on the scene with a rather unusual past. He'd begun his career as a campaign consultant for then–Westchester County District Attorney Jeanine Pirro, now a Fox News personality. She won reelection in November 1997, and Portale was hired by her office that December.

His employment there raised a few eyebrows since he had a questionable past—he'd been arrested twice in

Niagara Falls. The first arrest occurred on May 29, 1993, when he was at the Pleasuredome dance club and bar with Timothy O'Keefe. When an employee tried to eject O'Keefe for vandalizing the restroom, Portale had allegedly punched the employee in the eye. Ultimately, the charges were dismissed against both. The second time, he was charged with speeding, expired insurance, driving without a seat belt, and driving with an expired license. The violations were settled without a criminal charge.

After those two incidents, Portale went to Cleveland-Marshall College of Law and spent the following summer working for a lowly six dollars per hour as a law clerk for an attorney in Niagara Falls. Until he graduated from law school in 1997, he earned money as a beer vendor for the Cleveland Indians and, for a short time, as an assistant manager of the Fitness Shops in Lyndhurst, Ohio. Eventually, he settled in New York to work for Pirro and kept out of further trouble for four years, while he worked in the Westchester District Attorney's Youth Violence/Gang Unit. In his spare time, he played rugby and played it well, competing in the Empire State Games. In 1999, he was named to the USA National Rugby Team.

Then, in December 2001, he traveled to Florida to compete in a rugby tournament as a member of the semiprofessional New York Knights. He and his teammate Arlen Gerritson were arrested at the Days Inn in Tampa. According to the sheriff's office, the men had hired two exotic dancers but then decided they wanted sex. When the 18- and 25-year-old women insisted they were only there for dancing, Portale would not let them leave the room, leading to a charge of false imprisonment.

In addition, one of the women called her bodyguard and when he arrived an altercation broke out. Portale and Gerritson were both charged with battery. Portale's attorney, Anthony Quinn, said that the charges were an act of revenge against Portale for an accusation he'd made that the women's bodyguard had stolen items from his team-mates' rooms. Later, one of the alleged victims dropped her complaint and the charges were dropped.

The district attorney's office suspended Portale, but he continued to receive his $72,131 annual salary. He officially resigned from his position on January 14, 2002, and went into private practice. In 2015, he took on Ange-lika's case.

CHAPTER SEVENTEEN

On Mother's Day, according to *People* magazine, an individual visiting another jail inmate was disturbed by Angelika's attitude. "She doesn't look like she's mourning the death of someone she loved. To me, she's not well up there," she said, tapping a finger on her temple. She added that Angelika had flitted around wishing "Happy Mother's Day" to all visiting moms.

She talked about the tastiness of the food in jail and laughed uproariously with visiting friends. Was she making the best of a bad situation? Or did she actually like the place—and the media attention that accompanied her situation?

Portale came out swinging with his defense strategy, alleging that his client might be in jail illegally because of the state's inconsistency: he'd heard that she was indicted on May 5, then that she had not on May 8. He claimed the district attorney had first said murder in the second degree, then said it wasn't.

He demanded disclosure from the prosecution and filed

a request for a bail hearing with Judge Robert Freehill. On Wednesday, May 13, the parties gathered before the judge. Angelika stood at the defense table with three men: her lead attorney, Richard Portale; the balding, paler second attorney, Jeffrey Chartier; and the tall, beefy, brush-cut-topped forensic scientist Michael Archer, who loomed over the tiny defendant.

Chartier had worked in Westchester County as an assistant district attorney for ten years, before switching to private practice at the Law Offices of Murray Richman in 2007. He was best known for his defense of William Rockefeller, an engineer who fell asleep on a Metro-North Railroad train on December 1, 2013, causing it to jump the tracks. The resulting accident resulted in four deaths and more than seventy injuries. With Chartier's defense, focusing on the engineer's sleep apnea and a lack of proper track maintenance, no charges were brought against Rockefeller.

But Michael Archer appeared to be the defense's best weapon. His credentials included degrees in psychology, biology, forensic science, religious studies, and systemic theology. He also had teaching experience at Marist College in Poughkeepsie and at Mount Saint Mary College in Newburgh.

In the forensic science field, he'd worked on cases with well-known experts Dr. Henry Lee and Dr. Michael Baden. The case that brought him to prominence in his field was his role as lead forensic scientist for the defense team in the trial of Joran van der Sloot, charged with the murder of Natalee Holloway. During the case, Archer said, "There is no DNA or forensic evidence, there are no confessions, and there is no body. In the time Joran was with Natalee, it would be impossible for him to have killed her and disposed of her without leaving a trace. I am certain Joran did not kill Natalee Holloway." The judge agreed with Archer, and Archer was there for Joran's release from jail.

Unfortunately, he was now free to kill again, and he did. His murder of Stephany Flores Ramirez in 2010 resulted in a twenty-eight-year sentence in the prisons of Peru.

Now, at the prosecution's table, Assistant District Attorney Julie Mohl presented the state's case to the judge. She said that Angelika had told the detectives that "it felt good knowing . . . [Vince] would die." Her actions, Mohl said, proved this when she waited until Vince was underwater—a full twenty minutes after he capsized—before calling nine-one-one. "She stated that she tampered with the victim's kayak . . . she knew it would contribute to his death," Mohl added. "She felt trapped and it was her only way out." Mohl argued that Angelika was also motivated by greed, pointing to the life insurances policies. "She spoke to people about what she would do with the money," Mohl claimed.

Judge Freehill set bail at a staggering $3 million cash—an impossible amount for Angelika to raise. Between an online defense fund and her family and friends in Latvia scraping together all they could, she'd raised $120,000. A bail that high was too far a goal.

Alarm bells blared for Portale. He could not believe that he was hearing of this so-called confession two weeks after his client's arrest. "I'm skeptical of the statements," he said in a press conference after the hearing. He alleged that the language barrier was an issue in her interview with detectives and questioned whether her comments were voluntary. "She's very confident sounding and so even if she doesn't know what you're saying, she'll answer in an affirmative tone," Portale told reporters. As for her actions after the incident, he insisted that cultural differences had caused her to behave in a manner that appeared bizarre to Americans.

That same day, at 11:00 am, police recovered a male body from the Hudson River near a boathouse owned by

Marist College. Vince's family and friends were torn between hope and dread. An autopsy was scheduled for Thursday morning.

However, authorities soon released the news that it was not Vince's body. They did not release the identity of the dead man, nor would they give reporters any information about his age or ethnicity.

In Vince's circle, hope died another death and prayers went heavenwards to plead for the recovery of his body.

Ten long days later, their prayers were answered.

CHAPTER EIGHTEEN

On May 23, a short distance south of Bannerman Island, deputies from the Orange County Sheriff's Department lined the Hudson River at West Point U.S. Military Academy, keeping guard during the graduation ceremony for the class of 2015. A private boat glided along the water, its occupants enjoying a beautiful sunlit day. As the boaters neared the Cornwall Country Club, they stumbled upon a disturbing sight—a body floating facedown on the surface of the river. They rushed back to the law enforcement contingent at West Point and reported their gruesome discovery. The deputies kept watch until the state troopers arrived.

The body was pulled onto the dock at the country club. The deceased was a male, and the clothing he wore was very similar to what Vince Viafore had been wearing when he disappeared.

Senior Investigator Moscato felt a measure of relief at this discovery, for he knew the family would have a modicum of comfort now that they could bury Vince's body. The lingering belief in the possibility of a happy outcome had worn thin and grown fragile, but now it was crushed beneath the iron heel of fate. "I hated dashing the last bit of hope," Moscato reflected.

Echoing his sentiments, Mary Ann Viafore told CBS that the recovery of her son's body had filled her with conflicting emotions: "Sad that there was no hope. And happy that at least we found him and can bring him home."

Sean Von Clauss was devastated. He hadn't wanted to accept the reality of Vince's death, but once the body was found he could deny it no longer. Still, it didn't make sense. "Vinny had no malice towards anyone!" He contacted a medical professional to learn more about hypothermia, seeking to understand the last moments of his friend's life. "He told me that probably after four minutes in the water, Vinny started to lose motor skills. He said your lungs collapse after ten minutes in that temperature. It gives me chills just thinking about it."

On Tuesday, May 26, the first workday after the Memorial Day weekend, a medical examiner confirmed the identity of the body found on the Hudson River as that of 46-year-old Vincent Viafore.

That same day, the grand jury of Orange County handed down an indictment accusing Angelika Graswald of murder in the second degree. She also faced a second charge of manslaughter.

In a statement regarding the indictment, Orange County District Attorney David Hoovler said that Angelika had "yanked the drain plug from Viafore's kayak" and "moved the paddle away from him as he was struggling to stay afloat."

Portale mocked the charges, alleging that the accusation about the paddle was nothing but wishful thinking. He added that the removal of the plug would have had no impact on the vessel's buoyancy.

However, the state police did test their theory in multiple weather conditions, including videotaped evaluations under the exact conditions Vince had faced on April 19. They obtained the same model kayak as the one used by Vince and found a person of the same size to paddle. In calm water with the plug in place, the kayak did not take in any water. However, the kayak missing the plug took on water both in calm water and in tumultuous situations, without fail. Within eight to twelve minutes, the weight of the water in the vessel would cause it to submerge, regardless of the roughness of the sea.

That Friday, Angelika appeared in the Orange County Courthouse for her arraignment. Her hands were locked together in front of her body with handcuffs, her skin pale against the unflattering orange jumpsuit. Her long blond tresses were bound up in a bun. Her face betrayed no emotion. She uttered not a word as she stood between her lawyers, Richard Portale and Jeffrey Chartier.

Portale spoke for his client, submitting her not guilty plea to both charges. After the arraignment, he spoke to reporters: "We expect to see that this was accidental drowning, hypothermia, and possible acute alcoholic intoxication. I think it's pretty clear that they were drinking . . . at least had a couple of beers." Regarding the two charges of murder and manslaughter, he said, "Logically, a person can't commit the same act both intentionally and recklessly. [The prosecution is] . . . trying to fit a square peg into a round hole to make a homicide out of what is an accidental drowning." He added, "Miss Graswald is a victim here."

Since the last court date, the defense team had added an additional member, John Fleming, a retired Detective First Grade in the Intelligence Division. Prior to his work there, he'd gained investigative experience in the 1980s and

'90s working on homicide and robbery squads in the South Bronx and Harlem.

The McHoul Funeral Home in Hopewell Junction announced the funeral arrangements on June 9 in an obituary statement that began: "Vincent A. Viafore, a Poughkeepsie resident, was tragically taken from us on April 19, 2015. He was 46 years young."

The tribute continued with a short biography, followed by a more intimate portrait of the deceased: "He loved the Hudson River Valley and enjoyed running the Walkway on a regular basis while participating in various billiard and volleyball leagues, as well. He especially enjoyed spending time with his family and friends and had a very close relationship with his nephew, Michael."

The list of surviving family members included his ex-wife Suzanne but made no mention of his fiancée who was now sitting behind bars, charged with his murder. The announcement requested that news and media outlets not attend the services, out of respect to Vince's family.

On the day of the funeral, the prosecutors and defense attorneys stood before Judge Robert Freehill's bench. Freehill ordered both parties to refrain from speaking to the media or sharing any aspects of the case. This gag order was intended to limit publicity about developments and avoid polluting the jury pool. Despite the judge's intention, the silence didn't last long.

In many ways, Mary Ann Viafore remained oblivious to her surroundings at the funeral, numb from the pain, but she was aware enough to be shocked and warmed by the turnout for her son's service at St. Martin de Porres. She was surprised and overwhelmed when hundreds of people filled every seat in the pews and kept coming, stacking up between the pews and the back wall of the sanctuary. Her sorrow and pain were wrapped in a comforting blanket of love.

Bishop Dominick Lagonegro officiated at the mass. Laura Rice, in her eulogy, remembered her brother Vince as a "fun-loving" and bighearted brother who never hesitated to give a homeless person a few dollars or interrupt his day to take a little girl to get her bike fixed. "He tried to make everyone happy," she said. "Vinny will be missed every day and will never be forgotten. Remember Vinny enjoyed life every day to the fullest and would want us to do the same." She remembered his passion for volleyball, pool, and running. He also loved to cook and had mastered the art of smoked ribs—his "signature dish." She thanked Vince's large circle of friends, calling them "amazing." Laura ended her speech by saying, "From tragedy, I feel we need to find something good to help us go on. Without all of you, we never would have been able to continue moving forward." She urged his friends to do what Vince would want them all to do: "Let's celebrate his life." The audience greeted those words with an enthusiastic round of applause.

The solemn ritual of departure from the church to the waiting cars commenced, with the family members bound for the hearse. The procession traveled through Poughkeepsie, circling around multiple roundabouts, gliding past the stately grounds of Vassar College. The first vehicles turned onto La Grange and followed it to its dead end at Calvary Cemetery. Other cars grabbed the first empty spaces on adjacent roads and mourners walked the rest of the way.

At the cemetery, Mary Ann Viafore bid a final goodbye to her beloved son. Her pain was intense—no mother wants to survive her child. Her son's death felt like a life sentence as pieces of her heart lowered into the grave with the casket.

CHAPTER NINETEEN

On Thursday, July 9, 2015, Angelika Graswald appeared before Judge Freehill for a pretrial conference that centered on discovery issues. The defense presented a long list of the items they wanted from the state, including videos, still photographs, documents, and Angelika's diary. Often, discovery is a lengthy information-sharing process monitored by the trial judge.

The judge set three additional pretrial sessions for September 11, September 28, and October 16. The one piece of concrete information that both sides wanted was the autopsy report. They had two more months to wait.

On July 15, the defense sent Marc Janoson, a forensic psychologist, to perform an evaluation on Angelika. The state waited for the team to submit a notice of intent to present psychiatric evidence at trial. When the window to submit expired, they assumed they would never see one. Months later, they would learn they had been wrong.

CBS aired the *48 Hours* episode "Death on the Hudson" on July 29. The show included damaging excerpts from the recording of Angelika's police interrogation and Mike Colvin's reenactment of Angelika prostrating herself in his driveway in their argument over the couple's cat. Both clips strengthened the state's case against her. The audience heard her say she was "euphoric" when she realized Vince was going to die and "happy" and "relieved" when he was gone. They heard her tell police that Vince's sexual demands were over-the-top, as if a request for a threesome was a justifiable reason for homicide.

However, there were some interviews and demonstrations featured in the episode that supported Angelika's innocence. Michael Archer, the defense team's forensic expert, was ever present in the episode. He stated: "I haven't seen all the evidence, but the evidence I have seen certainly does not support homicide. This is, by all accounts, a tragic accident."

Archer introduced *48 Hours* correspondent Peter Van Sant to Buddy Behney, an operator of Mountain Top Outfitters, who crossed the river in a kayak just like Vince's with the plug removed. He traversed the span without incident. Then Archer conducted his own experiment. He sealed the cockpit of the kayak and removed the plug, then poured a full five-gallon bucket of water into the vessel. When he flipped it over, about an ounce of water came out. "For what wouldn't fill a shot glass, a woman is in jail being charged with murder," Archer said. The show made no mention of the state police's testing of the significance of the plug.

48 Hours followed up that attack on the prosecution with Jim Trainum, an interrogation expert who argued that he saw red flags in the interrogation video indicating that the so-called confession was coerced.

The prosecution didn't like the show at all. They were outraged that the defense had shared the police interrogation video with CBS.

* * *

The Orange County Medical Examiner released the autopsy report on September 10, reporting Vince's cause of death as drowning. The ME cited a two-inch abrasion on his body and bruises on his chest, arm, and left side, as well as a bloated face and abdomen marked by red and green discoloration. The toxicology indicated a blood alcohol level below the legal limit, at 0.066. None of these physical findings pointed to the manner of death; nonetheless, the report stated the means of Vince's death as homicide. The basis given for that conclusion was a "kayak drain plug intentionally removed by other."

The defense team was livid. "Clearly, the Orange County medical examiner failed to conduct any meaningful investigation of her own and relied on false information provided by the New York State Police," Portale said. "She ruled this a homicide without a scintilla of medical evidence."

A spokesperson for the county executive, Steven Neuhaus, came to the defense of Jennifer Roman, who'd performed the autopsy and written the report: "Obviously, the statute envisions that the autopsy is only one aspect of the medical examiner's report. If medical examiners were limited to basing their conclusions solely on a physical examination of the body, there would be no coroner inquests. The coroners and medical examiners have been doing this for over 100 years."

The family was relieved with the conclusion. They'd never believed that their loved one's death was an accident and now, they felt, the person responsible would pay for the wrong perpetrated against him.

As is often the case with a victim's family, any step in the dreary judicial process stirred up a pot of conflicting emotions. Vince's ex-wife Suzanne told *Newsweek,* "Unfortunately, I don't believe I'll ever have closure. Whatever happens, it's not going to bring Vinny back, but I'm really hoping for justice. I want . . . [Angelika] to spend the rest of her life in prison where she belongs. She should never get to hug her mother, sister, or friends, if she has any left, again."

On September 12, the parties gathered in Judge Freehill's courtroom again. The prosecution wanted a sample of Angelika's DNA to compare to evidence they possessed with an unknown genetic profile. The court granted the request and also granted Portale permission to be present when the buccal swab was taken from his client.

On the last day of September, the state filed an objection, claiming that the defense had violated the gag order by scheduling Angelika for a sit-down interview with ABC's *20/20* on October 1. They wanted the judge to protect the integrity of the case by ordering Graswald and Portale to stop making out-of-court statements. "Free speech is a balance. It must bend to the fair administration of justice," the state argued, adding that the proper place to try the case was in the courtroom, not in the press.

Portale admitted to pushing the envelope by providing videos to the media but insisted he was not violating any professional rules of conduct. Rather, he said, he was merely countering prejudicial information released during earlier press conferences. "The media has turned this into a confession when, in fact, after an eleven-hour interrogation, she didn't confess to killing Vincent Viafore. She never did."

Judge Freehill would not infringe on Angelika's First Amendment rights, but he forbade Portale from being present during the interview. "She has a right to sit down with a reporter and speak. Ms. Graswald must understand, she's damaging her own case, to a point." Turning to the defendant, he added, "You've got to be careful what you say."

When *20/20*'s Elizabeth Vargas sat down with Angelika, the reporter repeated that warning: "It can be a risky for a defendant like yourself to talk publicly before trial. Why did you decide to do this interview?"

"I needed a chance to let people know that I'm innocent. I'm being accused of murder, which I'm not capable of doing," Angelika told her. "I'm not a killer. I am a good person."

They talked together in the room normally used as the jail's chapel—it was where Angelika attended Bible study. The guards had allowed Angelika to wear a more flattering top over her orange jumpsuit.

Vargas turned the conversation to Angelika's remarks to law enforcement that she'd wanted to be "free" from Vince. "What I meant was I wanted to be free from the lifestyle that we had," Angelika explained. "The nightlife, strip clubs, the threesomes. I didn't want any part of that. I wanted to be free from that. But as far as he goes, I wanted to be with him."

CHAPTER TWENTY

A high-profile murder trial like Angelika's demanded funds beyond her reach, for attorneys, experts, testing, and other miscellaneous expenses. Her parents had scraped together whatever they could—even sending their life savings—and other members of her home community helped, too. Richard Portale started a campaign on Fund-Razr, "Justice for Angelika," with a goal of raising $75,000 for her defense. As of October 2015, only $270 had been raised.

Angelika's parents planted a tree in Latvia in Vince's memory and sent condolences to Vince's mother. In jail, Angelika attended classes, joined a Bible study group, and corresponded with her family, sending letters and artwork.

Sean Von Clauss sat in front of his television on the evening of November 6, 2015. He'd missed the *48 Hours* episode about the case and still entertained a speck of niggling doubt about Angelika's guilt. As he watched the show now for the first time, every shred of uncertainty melted away as he witnessed the toxicity of her words and attitude in the clips of her interrogation. "[I'm] disgusted and sick to my stomach," he said after the show ended. Later, he poured out his emotions in an email: "My worst nightmare is true! She admitted that she paddled away from Vinny. She said her 'demon' side told her not to help him. It's so unreal. I can't believe that little peanut could take away our beloved brother and friend. And in a cruel way. Freezing to death, only to drown. He must have been so horrified seeing her paddle away from him. I pray she didn't taunt him, but I'm sure she did—cursing him and laughing at him while he tried to stay afloat, clinging to his kayak freezing."

The tragic accident had had an enormous impact on Sean's life. "I can't sleep, and when I do, I keep waking up to Vinny screaming for her to help. I'm so sorry, Vinny. Almost every night, that same dream, of her taunting him and smiling as he is freezing and begging her to help. What a monster!"

After watching the episode, Sean had no more doubts about Angelika's guilt. "I know after hearing her statements that she did it. She planned it. She seduced him through sex and naughty pictures and she deliberately brought one life vest. That part of the interview has me troubled. She claims she didn't own any, but yet the day in question, Vinny said she should wear one? She planned it. I know it. Just can't prove it. I personally think once she knew of the $250,000 insurance, she started plotting."

Over in Surrogate Court in Dutchess County, Laura Rice filed a request that Angelika be prohibited from collecting Vince's insurance money or any of his assets. The document stated that the family intended to file a wrongful death suit. Judge James Pagones signed an order to that effect on November 20, 2015, blocking any payouts from the State Farm and Zurich American life insurance policies.

In court, Angelika usually allowed the attorneys to do all the talking. Back in Freehill's court for another pretrial hearing on December 21, Angelika finally spoke up. With a smile on her face, she wished the judge a Merry Christmas.

The judge, however, had more pressing matters on his mind. He complained to the lawyers on both sides of the courtroom that "the currents [weren't] moving too swiftly in this case." Observers wondered what actions he would take to accelerate the trial.

The next step in the pretrial dance was scheduled and rescheduled several times, but finally everyone returned to the courtroom on February 25, when Judge Freehill responded to several motions from the defense. Portale and Chartier had objected to all ten search warrants issued in the case. However, the court ruled that the defense lacked standing to challenge the two warrants for two cell-phone records and the three for Facebook, Apple iCloud, and Yahoo.

The defense had also requested that the indictment against their client be dismissed or that the charges be reduced. The judge ruled against them on both.

A number of motions remained, including the most pivotal one: the defense's desire for a Huntley Hearing, a pretrial review of the manner in which the police had obtained statements from the defendant. In this proceeding, the judge must determine if the responses by the defendant were voluntary beyond a reasonable doubt. If he decided otherwise, the state could not submit that evidence to the jury at trial.

Portale wanted all eleven hours of interrogation video suppressed, along with the statements made by Angelika the night of the incident and at the barracks on April 28 and on the island on April 29. This evidence was vital to the state's case. If the judge ruled in favor of the defense, no one was certain if the prosecutors could move forward. Freehill scheduled the hearings for May 2, 2016, more than a year after Angelika's arrest.

CHAPTER TWENTY-ONE

Of course, the May date for the hearing did not stand. This delay was caused by one of Portale's clients, whose trial started April 26. Angelika's hearing was rescheduled for June 6, 2016.

A Huntley Hearing was specific to the state of New York, but the legal precept was common, though referred to by other names in different state courtrooms. This type of court procedure exists to determine the admissibility of evidence, including confessions. The practice was established following a 1965 New York Appeals Court decision that brought the state into accordance with a U.S. Supreme Court ruling the year before.

The issues considered by judges during a Huntley Hearing included whether or not the individual was in custody at the time of the statement, if Miranda Rights were appropriately waived, and if the defendant had made his comments of his or her own free will. The judge needed to rule on the voluntariness based on the beyond-reasonable-doubt standard.

In many cases, a confession could be considered nothing more than the icing on the evidentiary cake. It can be used to corroborate witness testimony or forensic evidence such as fingerprints, DNA, blood spatter, or other concrete items. In the Graswald case, however, the confession was the linchpin of the state's argument. No witnesses existed. No fingerprints were relevant. No blood evidence was left behind. Without the words from Angelika's lips, the prosecutors had only flimsy circumstantial evidence that would be unlikely to convince jurors of her guilt.

For that reason, the outcome of the hearing was vital for both sides in the courtroom, and it all rested in Judge Freehill's hands. On the one hand, without Angelika's statements to law enforcement the possibility that the state would prevail and secure a guilty verdict were minimal at best and the defense's chances of a win were magnified tenfold. On the other hand, if the judge found the taped interview admissible, the impact of Angelika's words and behavior during the interview had the potential to swing a jury to a guilty verdict. The dramatic import of the Huntley Hearing was staggering.

On June 6, a harsh tone of contention dominated Judge Freehill's courtroom. To begin, the defense complained about what they'd requested and had not received from the state. In all likelihood, they knew full well the reasons for any delay or denial in the delivery of materials, but Portale and Chartier were playing the victim card in hopes of manipulating the judge. The state responded that some of the requested recordings did not exist and others no longer existed because they were temporary in nature.

The defense seemed to believe that if they could get wins on the other pending motions, they might swing the judge's thinking to their point of view on the Huntley issue. Despite knowing that the Huntley hearing was the basis for that day's court appearance, they attempted to argue other outstanding motions, including a motion to reargue, instigating a heated exchange with Freehill.

"In that motion to reargue," the judge said, "I don't believe that there was anything brought up about the Huntley Hearing issue, and that's what we're going to proceed with today. And then there will be a subsequent decision on your motion to reargue. I'm ready to proceed with a Huntley Hearing. I've heard enough."

Portale tried to delay the proceedings by pushing the court into a hearing on a different motion altogether. The judge blocked his attempt. Chartier stepped up to the plate, pitching the possibility of constitutional issues over the unreasonable search or seizure of Angelika's possessions, and Angelika's inability to leave police custody before she'd been arrested. "I'm just trying to streamline this," he argued.

"No, you're not, Mr. Chartier," the judge snapped. "It doesn't appear to me you're trying to streamline this. I'm ready to proceed with the Huntley Hearing and that's what we're gonna do. Any motions you want to make, we can continue them later."

Portale pushed again, telling the judge that the second issue mentioned by Chartier went "hand in hand with the Huntley issue."

"I'm having the hearing first. I'm not deciding at this point."

With all the other legal issues set aside by the judge, the Huntley Hearing began.

ADA Julie Mohl called the first witness: Officer Stephen Bedetti of the Town of New Windsor Police Department and the Town of Cornwall Police Department, one of the first responders to the river on April 19, 2015. Bedetti described his initial encounter with the defendant in the rescue boat, onshore, and at the ambulance. He said he had not introduced himself to Angelika by name, but he'd been wearing a uniform and she knew he was with the police.

Bedetti related what Angelika had told him about that afternoon's kayak trip, the loss of her cell phone, her possession of the car keys, and his aborted attempt to search for the phone in her backpack.

"How did you end your conversation with the defendant?" ADA Mohl asked.

"She asked me to bring her back to her car."

"How was her demeanor when you were speaking to her, at the landing?"

"Calm, very. I mean, like you and I are talking right now."

"And how was her demeanor at the hospital?"

"A little anxious to get out of there, honestly. She didn't want to be there anymore."

"When you were speaking to her, Officer, did you have trouble understanding anything that she said?"

"No," he said, shaking his head.

"Did she ever ask you to clarify anything that you said to her?"

"No, not once."

"And when you were speaking, were her answers appropriate to your questions and to the conversation you were having?"

"Yeah, I was getting it."

"And, Officer, this may sound like a silly question, but what language were you two conversing in?"

"English."

"The whole time?"

"Yes."

After the prosecutor had completed her questioning, she turned the witness over to the defense. Before starting,

Portale asked for a moment to review material he'd received that morning and said, "Judge, may I? While I review this, Miss Graswald is in chains, her hands are in chains, her waist is in chains, her legs are in chains. Could she be unchained for the purposes of this hearing?"

"Her hands can be," the judge allowed.

"Thank you," Portale said. He then submitted a handful of defense exhibits, labeled "L," "M," "N," and "O." He walked the witness through his professional career, first as a dispatcher, followed by sixteen years with the New Windsor Police Department as a patrolman.

Portale then drew Bedetti's attention to exhibit L. "Are those your handwritten notes?" he asked.

"They are."

"Do you recall where you were when you took those notes?

"At St. Luke's Hospital."

"And you had a notebook?"

"I did not," Bedetti said. He explained that his notebook had been in his partner's car and that he'd used his ticket book card instead.

"When you responded to the call relating to this case, did you think to grab a notebook?"

"No," Bedetti said. "I'm a volunteer fireman. I know seconds save lives. So, I figured the fastest I got there, the fastest I would be able to help out. If I had to jump in the water or something or get on a boat. So, no, that was the furthest thing from my mind."

The defense attorney then presented exhibit O, the incident report Bedetti had submitted. "When did you fill that out?"

"I actually filled out most of that report that night when I came back. And then after learning the, I guess I'm gonna call it, the victim's name later on down the road, I actually edited the report. I had to put his real name in there.

It was wrong. I had put him in there as Victor and I guess it was Vincent. So, I went back in and added it. I indicated the date I edited it."

Portale moved on to Bedetti's comments about Angelika's behavior the night of the accident.

"You testified on direct about my client's demeanor. Do you recall that? And you were making some opinions about her demeanor?"

"No, well, I just stated the facts, what I observed."

"What did you observe?"

"She [was] like you and I are talking right now," the police officer said.

"What does that mean?" Portale asked.

"Just matter-of-fact. Not—didn't show any emotion. Just oddly acting."

"You were aware that the individual she was kayaking with was still missing, correct, yes?"

"You know, I think I [could] only guess at that point, because I know there was a rescue boat that had come back and I know there was other people out in the river. So, at that point, could he have been picked up? Yeah, I'm sure he could. I wasn't with the command post and everything at that point because I was talking to her. So, to sit here and say I was actually aware that he was missing at the point, I could just only assume that he was."

"And she was the only person that you encountered, out of the two people in the kayak?"

"She was the last one with him, yes."

Portale then badgered him about the water temperature and his lack of knowledge about Angelika's medical condition after being rescued. Bedetti, however, insisted repeatedly that he had no knowledge of the water temperature, since he had never gone into the river, and was unaware of any medical diagnosis or treatment.

For some reason, Portale just couldn't let go of that

question. "So the answer was that you don't know what she was being treated for."

"I have no idea what her actual medical treatment was, no."

"So, if I ask you a yes or no question, do you think you could try to answer it with a yes or no?" Portale said dryly.

"Sure."

"Okay, great. In your sixteen years on the job as a police officer, have you encountered people who have been suffering from hypothermia before?"

"Yes."

"About how many times?"

"Maybe two or three," Bedetti answered. "That's just in my police career."

"What are the symptoms of hypothermia, if you know?"

"It depends on how long you are in there, yes, but I mean, obviously, it's very cold, confused, palish. I guess some people could react differently than others, but I have never encountered this type of hypothermia."

"What type is that?" Portale asked, his exasperation evident in the arch of his eyebrows.

"Just like you and I are talking right now."

"You have never encountered it?"

"I have never seen it, no."

"And have you encountered, in your sixteen years as a police officer, individuals who had just experienced a loss, a tragic loss?"

"Oh, yes," Bedetti said.

"Are you aware of the stages of grief?"

"Yeah. I mean, I would say that I have seen people who have lost people in front of them or—"

Portale interrupted. "My question is: Are you aware of the stages of grief?"

"I don't know the actual terms of them, no. I wouldn't know that. I just know, me being a human, how I react."

"You know how you react?" Portale asked skeptically.

"Uh-huh."

"So, when you were describing Miss Graswald's demeanor, you were describing it and judging it as you would react, correct?"

"No. As I've seen other people react."

"But you're not familiar with the different stages of grief?"

"The actual ones in the book, no, I can't say that I am."

"Have you investigated homicides before?"

"Can't say that I have."

"So, this would have been your first homicide, correct?"

"I didn't know it—I went there for a missing person that was in a kayak. So, I—the case was not—it turned over to the state police or the state police took it, so I can't say that [it] really would have been."

"But, at the time, you [had] never investigated a homicide, correct?"

"Never [had]."

"Okay. So, this would have been your first homicide, yes?"

ADA Julie Mohl rose to her feet. "Objection, Judge."

"He gave an answer, Mr. Portale. Sustained."

Portale then took Bedetti step by step through the dispatch process that brought him to the river that night, questioning the officer's responses as if he doubted every word. His tone of voice and abrupt movements made his impatience obvious. Portale established that although the patrol sergeant sent him to the river, the officer had gone to the hospital on his own.

Then Portale asked, "When you wrote the supporting deposition we talked about, that's Defendant's N for identification, what did you use to help your memory in writing that deposition?"

"My brain," Bedetti said. "I was at home when it happened. They came to my house and did it, the investigators."

"Did you have your notes?"

"I had nothing. They just pulled in my driveway and there I was doing the lawn."

Portale turned to the name Victor that Bedetti had originally written in his incident report. The lawyer hassled him for saying that Angelika gave him that name at the hospital.

After that, the defense attorney nitpicked the details of each encounter the officer had had with Angelika. He posed accusatory questions about why Bedetti was asking his client questions instead of helping her get off the boat or get on the gurney. Portale was doing everything he could to make Bedetti appear to be a non-caring oaf.

The police officer defended himself as best as he could, pointing to the fact that she had been able to walk and talk and seemed to be medically sound. He insisted that he had stopped questioning her once the paramedics began checking her vitals.

The lawyer moved on to the ringing phone Bedetti had heard at the dockside, ridiculing the officer's inability to replicate the sound. "What else, if anything, did you do to locate that phone?"

The officer explained that the Cornwall Police Department had a screen capture of the original 911 call and were attempting to call the phone to see if they could find it. "My concern at that point is, if she had the phone, if it was in the river with her . . . we can attempt to get a ping on it, so we can locate a smaller area of a recovery or rescue location."

"My question to you is: What did you do *physically* at

that time to locate the phone that you heard ringing at the foot of the gurney?"

"I went down and picked her life vest up. I verbally said, 'Whose phone is ringing?' and no one responded. And like I testified, the female paramedic looked at me, I don't know, awkward [like] she doesn't understand what I'm looking to do."

"Move to strike what she thought," Portale snapped.

"I'm not going to strike that, for the record," said the judge. "Continue."

"I picked up the life vest and the minute I picked the life vest up, Miss Graswald, who was laying on the gurney, sat up. Almost like I had a string attached to the life vest and her. She sat up. I looked at it real quick, inspected it, and I kind of looked over at her. And now she is being distracted, if you will, from being medically checked out. So I put the life vest back down and then she laid back down."

Portale's badgering didn't end there. He ferreted for additional details about Bedetti's search for the phone on the scene, for the definition of "command post," and whether his vehicle or another was the command post. Then he questioned Bedetti about the location of the gurney, its height and its length, and the distance from Angelika's hands to the life vest.

The defense attorney then addressed why Bedetti had decided to follow Angelika to the hospital. "She had stated that the phone was in the river. But you had heard what you thought was her phone ringing. That didn't add up to you, correct?"

"Weird," Bedetti affirmed.

"And so, for that and other reasons, you wanted to go to the hospital and try to straighten it out. What were some of the other reasons you were suspicious?"

"Just a general reaction, after witnessing somebody

perhaps disappear in front of your eyes. [To] come back very matter-of-fact. Picking the life vest up, her sitting up. And then laying back down. Then, at the hospital, just wanting to ask me how long before hypothermia set in."

"Because of these reasons that you just stated, you went to the hospital to question her further?"

"Yes. Because she was the last one seen with somebody. Somebody needs to go speak to her and talk to her and find out, because there [were] so many people and it was confusing. At this point, there's three agencies: the state police, the Cornwall police, New Windsor police, the New Windsor side, all involved. And I got to be quite honest with you. I'm one of them no-nonsense, 'let's get down to the hospital and figure it out, while you're all gonna sit there and figure out who's gonna take it over.'"

Asked for further explanation, Bedetti continued, "The river's a touchy situation with everybody, as far as geographical area. You know, the center line of it. Dutchess County. It gets monotonous."

After more tedious badgering, including senseless questioning of whether or not the black bag actually qualified as a purse or not, Bedetti was temporarily released for the lunch recess. In all likelihood, the police officer was probably hoping for a miracle to keep him from having to return to the witness stand. Unfortunately, he didn't get one.

After recess, court resumed with ADA Julie Mohl objecting repeatedly that Portale's questions had been asked and answered prior to the lunch break. The judge sustained some of them, but not all. Portale continued plowing well-tilled territory, obviously attempting to keep the witness off balance.

The defense attorney badgered him about the exact location of where he'd placed Angelika's vest, stepping on Bedetti's answers every time he spoke. Mohl objected to his interruptions.

Freehill told Portale, "It's not a yes or no answer. Let him elaborate."

"Try it," Portale said to Bedetti.

"I picked the vest up. When I picked the vest up, like at the scene, Mrs. Graswald sat back up. Hear me out," the officer pleaded when he noticed Portale preparing to interrupt.

"Objection," Portale barked. "Move to strike. I want to know where he put them."

"Judge, he asked the question," the assistant district attorney said.

"He is answering the way he wants to answer it," Portale complained. "I ask you to instruct him to please tell me where he put them."

"I believe he's doing so," the judge said.

"He actually is not. He's actually trying to—"

"I'm trying—" Bedetti said.

"I think he is," Freehill said, "so, overruled."

"I'm trying," the police officer said. "I can answer?"

"You can continue," the judge responded.

"Withdrawn," Portale said, and then asked, "Where did you put the clothes?"

"Go ahead," the judge encouraged the witness.

"So, when I picked the vest up, she leaned forward again—"

"Objection!" Portale exclaimed. "Move to strike."

"I'm not striking that," Freehill said.

"I put the vest down. It was next to where—"

"Withdrawn," Portale said again. "Was there a location in the room where you placed the clothes, yes or no?"

"I need to explain," Bedetti plead.

"Just because you don't like the way the answer is going, you don't get to withdraw your question," the judge reprimanded the defense attorney.

"I don't like his answer," Portale said. "And I don't like

the ruling either. So, I'm withdrawing the question and asking a new question."

"I don't believe you can do that," Judge Freehill said. The court reporter read back the question and Freehill instructed the witness to "go from there."

"So, when I picked up the vest, Mrs. Graswald sat up like she did at the scene. I look at the vest real quick. Now I don't know if she is sitting up because I have the vest in my hand, or if she is fixated on this bag on the floor. So, I simply took that vest and put it on the other side of the chair. So now I can make eye contact with her, to see which one is more concern to her or not. Put the vest back down, which was probably a foot away from where it originally was. That's moving on the other side of the room or across the room or what—it was about a foot. Then I picked up the bag for her and handed her the bag."

The judge told Portale to ask his next question. The lawyer decided to quibble with the witness about his description of "across the room." When he didn't like the officer's answer, he turned sarcastic. "Did you learn that in your training at the police academy?"

The judge sustained the prosecutor's objection to that remark.

Portale continued, "Did you testify on direct that you asked Miss Graswald whether or not she was using or [she] and Vincent were using some waterproof equipment or material or something?"

"Uh-huh."

"What does that mean?" Portale asked.

"Yes or no," the judge prompted the witness.

"Could you just, rather than nodding or saying 'uh-huh,' could you just say yes or no?" the attorney parroted.

"My apologies," Bedetti said.

"Okay," Portale said.

The judge was not pleased. "I thought I took care of that, Mr. Portale."

"I was trying to help you."

"I don't need help," the judge said.

"I'm a helper. I'm sorry." Bedetti explained that he wanted to know if Angelika had a waterproof container with her, hoping she did and the phone was in it and still functional. Then he answered, "Uh-huh," again. Once more the judge said, "Yes or no."

"Yes. I apologize. My bad. Yes," the embarrassed witness responded.

Portale had the gall to ask the judge, "Do you need my help?"

"I do not," was the judge's terse response.

Portale proceeded in his attempts to make Bedetti look foolish for not having his Miranda Rights card with him in the courtroom and for the error corrections on his original report.

Then questions moved to the timeline that Angelika had given him on April 19, 2015. Portale pressed him about the accuracy of the times in his notes and the times he stated on the stand. After that, he turned to questions about any state police he talked to at the scene. Bedetti reminded him, "The fire department is actually in charge at that time, not the police. This was actually a recovery mission, so the fire department is actually in charge."

Finally, the defense released the witness. On redirect, the prosecution established that Bedetti had never put Angelika in handcuffs, had never put her under arrest, and never saw her again after that evening.

CHAPTER TWENTY-TWO

The state then called Trooper Andrew Freeman to the stand. He had worked for the New York State Police for three and a half years and was working the 7:00 pm to 7:00 am shift on the evening of April 19, 2015. He reported to the Cornwall Yacht Club after the 911 call and was sent to the Cornwall branch of St. Luke's Hospital. He was re-routed from there to the Newburgh location. He testified that he had spoken to Angelika briefly before Investigator DeQuarto arrived.

"And once Officer DeQuarto arrived, did there come a time that the defendant left the hospital?" Mohl asked.

"Yes, ma'am. I transported her from the hospital to the state police barracks in Montgomery." He added that she'd sat in the front seat next to him and they'd talked about her harrowing experience on the river.

ADA Mohl went through the same series of questions she'd asked Bedetti regarding Angelika's demeanor, the absence of handcuffs, the language spoken, and the level of comprehension on both sides. Freeman's answers echoed Bedetti's on every point.

"Did she ever ask you for an attorney while you were speaking to her in the car?"

"No, ma'am."

"Did she ever tell you that she didn't want to discuss what happened with you?"

"No, ma'am."

"Once you arrived back at the state police headquarters in Montgomery, what did you and Miss Graswald do, where did you go?"

"To the BCI offices. And then I left the station and I went back to the scene."

"After that point, Trooper Freeman, have you had any contact with her since your conversations with her on April 19?"

"No, ma'am."

"Did you discuss with her how many times, if any, she had kayaked out to Bannerman's Island?"

"She said this was the first time, with Mr. Viafore."

"So, this is the first time the two of them had gone out to Bannerman?"

"From what she told me, ma'am, yes."

Unlike the previous cross-examination, Portale's questions to the trooper were fairly straightforward and were answered in kind. The defense repeated many of the queries presented by the state. The lawyer was curious to know if Freeman had spoken to Bedetti after he'd given his testimony that morning. If the defense wanted to demonstrate collusion between witnesses, Freeman's response that he'd told the officer where he could find his lunch stopped that line of accusation as quickly as it started. Freeman showed no signs that he was intimidated by the defense.

Moving on, ADA Mohl called Aniello Moscato to the stand. Moscato began his career with the New York State Police in 1986. He became an investigator in 1994 and was promoted and assigned to the Montgomery barracks as a senior investigator in 2004.

On April 19, 2015, Moscato was not on duty, but he reported to Cornwall Landing that night at about 9:00 nonetheless. Shortly after his arrival and discussions with the Cornwall Police Department, the state police took charge of the investigation.

As Moscato took his seat facing the courtroom, an intimidating air of authority and command surrounded him like a shield. The animation in his eyes, however, showed a more lighthearted side of the man beneath the tough exterior. If you met him at a backyard barbecue, he'd seem more like an Italian teddy bear with a booming infectious laugh.

ADA Mohl began, "As part of your investigation, starting when you first arrived on the nineteenth of April, did you have conversations with Angelika Graswald?"

"Yes. On the nineteenth, I did not speak to Angelika. However, for the following day and for the following nine days, on and off, I had many conversations with her. We met with Angelika on the shores and in an attempt to try to locate Vincent Viafore."

"You spoke to her in person?"

"Yes, I did."

"Did you also speak to her over the phone?"

"Yes, I did."

"Did other members of your agency as well?"

"Yes, they did."

"Over the course of that ten days, did there ever come a point where Angelika refused to speak to you?" Mohl asked.

"No, not at all. She was very cooperative. And we became friends in that short period of time," Moscato admitted. "My heart felt for her, as it did for the Viafore family."

"Objection," Portale said. "Move to strike as non-responsive."

Stone-faced, the judge said, "Overruled. Denied. Continue."

Mohl took Moscato through the details of the arrangements he'd made for the use of the boat on April 29, 2015. Then the testimony moved to a discussion of that day's events.

After getting Moscato to identify Angelika in the courtroom, she asked, "What did you do once you got off of the boat?"

"Well, like I said before, we wanted to go there to take a look around since nobody [had] been there since the nineteenth. And we took a look around the island, just for any kind of clues as to what maybe might have transpired and what could have happened. Before then, Angelika had told us that she had been on the island for quite some time with Vincent. So, we thought it would be a good idea to see if, maybe—she missed telling us something, or we overlooked something. So, we wanted to be thorough. And we needed to check the entirety of the island."

Moscato told the court about Angelika's arrival on the island and his request for her to walk investigators through the last six hours she had spent with Vince.

"Did the defendant agree to go through these steps and explain those things to you?" Mohl asked.

"She did . . . she did. But, you know, obviously she was upset about everything going on. And she seemed a little bit uneasy. And I had to ask her to focus a couple of times and listen. . . . She had a hard time focusing on just a simple thing like 'where did you dock the kayaks when you came over?' She [was] pacing back and forth."

When she finally showed him the spot, Moscato was troubled. "What concerned me about where she said she had parked is that the guide wires were only about a foot above the level of the water," he explained. "And it's on a floating dock. So, regardless of the tide being in or out, it would be that same one foot. Nonetheless, she said that's where she parked the kayaks and they got out."

"Did you note anything about her behavior when you were talking to her on the dock that stood out to you?"

"Like I said, she was uneasy. She was pacing back and forth. She kept holding her stomach like it was upset. And she just had a hard time focusing. She had a very hard time focusing, but she had been through a lot, so, kind of understandable. And, you know, we, like I said, for the last nine days we met almost on a daily basis and we got to know each other. So, it was an amicable situation there. It wasn't adversarial in any way. And, remember, you got to keep in mind, we still, nine days later, hadn't found Vincent's body. So we were concerned about finding his body."

When Angelika started talking about her personal relationship with Vince, Moscato explained, he figured the topic was better suited for a one-on-one conversation. "I know that they were fiancés—but we were treating her like the grieving widow. We didn't want to make it seem like anybody is ganging up on her, or anything like that. So I asked her would you prefer just to talk to one of us." He said that she went off with Investigator DeQuarto and he and DaSilva "went off to the side there where the castle is. There is a bench near by there. And Investigator DaSilva and I went and we sat down on that bench for the duration of the conversation that Angelika and Investigator DeQuarto had on the path."

"Do you know how long that you and Investigator DaSilva were sitting on the bench?" Mohl asked.

"I would say probably about forty minutes or so, give or take."

"And after that duration of time, did you see Investigator DeQuarto and the defendant again?"

"Yes, I saw them walking towards us from that path that I just described. And I saw Angelika go down towards the dock where the bathroom was at. And Investigator De-Quarto came over to me."

"So, the defendant was able and allowed to walk to the bathroom on her own?"

"Oh, absolutely," Moscato confirmed.

"No one followed her?"

"No one followed her."

He reiterated the information DeQuarto had relayed to his colleague about the kayak plug and the paddle ring and described the boat ride back to the mainland.

"Did she ever ask not to get on the boat?"

"No, not at all. In fact, we had some engine problems with the boat, so we were joking a little bit back and forth."

"Did any further conversation about the plug or the ring come up while you were on the boat?"

"No, not at all."

"Did you have a conversation on the boat with the defendant other than when you were joking about?"

"No, that was about it. That it was kind of windy. And we joked a little bit around the boat issues and that was it, no, no further conversations occurred."

"Did you notice anything she was doing while she was on the boat?"

"Well, she was, I don't know how to explain it, but she wasn't—she wasn't visibly upset about anything. It was almost like she was happy-go-lucky. And, you know, I was a little taken aback, but I didn't say anything to her at that point. That, you know, after she just had said what she said to Investigator DeQuarto, that she would have this happy-go-lucky attitude. So we kind of just left it at that."

In response to the ADA's questions, Moscato told the court that he rode in his own vehicle back to the barracks while Angelika rode with the other two investigators. The only additional conversation he had with her was a brief one as they were entering the barracks, when Angelika commented on her desire to go motorcycling.

The prosecution turned the witness over to the defense and Portale asked for a break to review a document. Instead, the judge broke for the day and ordered the parties to return the next day at 1:30 pm.

CHAPTER TWENTY-THREE

On the second day of proceedings, lead defense attorney Richard Portale began the cross-examination of Senior Investigator Aniello Moscato. He focused first on the lead sheets generated in the investigation—logs that keep track of when new lines of investigation are opened in a case. The attorney tried to imply that the police started looking into Angelika as a suspect on April 19, 2015, because that date was on the lead sheet. Even after Moscato informed him that the date on the forms referred to the incident date, not when the form was filled out, Portale kept pushing.

"In reference to the lead sheets," Moscato explained, "that did not commence until the evening of the twenty-ninth. We tried to start treating this as a major crime investigation after the arrest was made, not prior to the arrest."

"Are you aware that there is a lead sheet dated 4/19/15 by Trooper Freeman, that says the lead was assigned by you?" Portale pressed.

"That's right," the investigator said. "And that probably wasn't assigned till the twenty-ninth. Do you see where the lead was reviewed and completed on the bottom? It should reflect. The lead may have been assigned on the twenty-ninth and it reflected what was done on the nineteenth. That is very much possible."

Portale moved on. "So, you were first assigned to this case on April 19; is that right?"

"Yes. I wasn't technically assigned," Moscato clarified again. "I'm the supervisor. And I was called in. And because of the nature of what it was, I responded down to Cornwall Yacht Club on the nineteenth."

"So, because you're a supervisor, you didn't really get assigned, you were 'the guy:' is that fair to say?"

"I guess," Moscato said, giving the attorney an incredulous look.

"You can say it. It's okay."

"I don't know if I'm 'the guy,' but yes, I responded. My squad is out there. Some of my guys were out there. I like to go and give them support and try to help facilitate things that needed to be done."

The men discussed the various local police, emergency response, and fire department members Moscato talked to that night, as well as the investigator's almost daily contact with Angelika before her arrest. "We might have missed a day in between, but we at least met up on the shores of the Hudson in one way or another," Moscato said. "And we either spoke on the phone or we texted each other. I believe she texted me more than I texted her back, but to this day, she's still on my cell phone as Angelika."

Portale established that Moscato hadn't been present for the meeting Angelika had with DeQuarto on the nineteenth and that Moscato had listened to the 911 call with DeQuarto sometime prior to April 29. "Did he make you aware of the fact that he was suspicious of Miss Graswald after listening to that call?"

"Suspicious?" Moscato asked.

"Yes."

"No. Listen, Angelika went through a lot in the first couple of days. Everyone reacts to these situations in different ways."

"Objection," Portale said, "to the non-responsive part of the question and move to strike it. It was a yes or no question."

"I'll sustain the objection," Judge Freehill said.

A flash of exasperation crossed Moscato's face.

"Are you okay?" Portale asked him.

"I'm fine," a clearly provoked Moscato said. The expression on his face and his curt responses to the next few questions said otherwise. He had to elaborate, though, when asked about his reaction to DeQuarto's statement about Angelika admitting she'd removed the kayak's plug.

Portale asked, "Is it fair to say that part of the reason you found that hard to believe and that you were in shock was that she was acting happy-go-lucky? That was your testimony [on] direct?"

"That's not the reason," Moscato contradicted. He continued with a lengthy answer that seemed to be daring Portale to object. "Number one, I didn't know about a plug. So that was surprising to me. And, also, like I was trying to say, for nine to ten days we were all on an emotional roller coaster, more so for the family and Angelika than myself. I kind of felt the pain they were experiencing. And she was being treated like a widow, if you will. A grieving widow. So, I was totally shocked that, you know, because of certain actions and behaviors that she exhibited before? I didn't really put a lot of weight on that. I'm sure you heard she would do cartwheels.

"In fact, on that Friday before, she called me up and she invited me to a nightclub. Said, 'Hey, what are you guys doing?' Like, 'We're down at the Hudson River. We're searching for Vinny's body.' And she's like, 'Oh, it's too cold out there. Aniello, why don't you tell the guys to take the rest of the day off and we're gonna have a little tribute to Vinny.' I forget the name of the place, but it was across the river on the Poughkeepsie side. She said that it was a tribute to Vinny. And she wanted all of the people that were assisting with the search to join her at the party.

"So, you know, a lot of people are, well, 'that's kind of odd.' But was it odd? Yeah, maybe. But you know what? Everybody grieves differently. Some people hide it. Some people are happy about it. Some people are sad about it. You know, everyone acts differently. So, I didn't put a lot of weight on that.

"Over the thirty-some years of doing this type of missing persons, and unnatural deaths, homicides, call it what you want—when a loved one's lost, people's reactions have been the spectrum of the rainbow. Anything is possible. You can't go to a textbook and say, 'This is what they should be doing.' So, I didn't put a lot of weight on her doing cartwheels and being happy about everything. Maybe others did, but I didn't."

If Portale was affected by Moscato's impassioned response, he didn't show it. "Yesterday when you testified that you were surprised that she was acting happy-go-lucky on Bannerman's Island, what did you mean?"

"Absolutely, I did. This is after she tells Investigator DeQuarto that she pulled the plug and sabotaged the paddle. How could you act happy-go-lucky after making a statement like that? It wasn't consistent with what she had just revealed . . . yes. That I was taken aback on."

"She wasn't acting like someone that had just confessed to murder; is that fair to say?"

"That's fair to say," Moscato conceded.

Portale asked the investigator to describe his actions on the morning of April 29. "Describe what you and your crew did, from the time you arrived to the time she arrived,

what did you do—start with you. What did you personally do?"

"Okay. We looked around the island. We spoke to some
people there that were on the cleanup committee. Some
were planting flowers, others were just cleaning up. And
we just, we looked around for any kind of evidence—keep
in mind, at this point, we still had not found Vincent Viafore's body. So, we were concerned that maybe something may have happened on the island. We weren't sure.
Maybe something was left behind on the island. You
know, the whole issue that there was a cell phone involved.
Maybe some pictures that were taken. Maybe some ar-
ticles of clothing might have been left behind. Whatever.
We had never been to Bannerman's Island since this incident had occurred. So, we were there to kind of take a first
look at it, if you will."

"So, this incident happened on the nineteenth. In the ten
days that followed, you, before the twenty-ninth, you had
never been to the island."

"That's right," the investigator said. "And that's why we
made it a point to go out there. You are absolutely right.
You know, we were busy concentrating on the scuba
searches, you had the shore searches, based on the information that we had. And as time went by and Vincent's
body didn't surface, we wanted to expand the search, if you
will. That maybe he got hung up on some of the rocks on
the other side of the island, what have you, and [we] wanted
to try to re-create what happened."

"You just testified that you were concerned that something may have happened on the island, correct?"

"Yes."

"You mean like foul play?"

"Not necessarily, no," Moscato hedged.

"Well, what do you mean?"

"Well, I know what I know now, but back then I—"

"What do you mean 'back then'?"

"Back then, well, I knew Angelika had spent some time on the island with Vincent Viafore. And she had taken some pictures. And I don't know the extent of all the pictures, but some of the descriptions that she had offered to the investigators and myself were to the effect that they were there enjoying the day and sharing some intimate moments with each other. I don't know if she—I think I do know, but I don't know exactly—but she brought a change of clothing and they took some photographs [with] some, if you will, some sexy poses and lingerie. So, perhaps, maybe something was left behind. It was part of our duty to be thorough and take a look to see if we missed something. Not necessarily foul play, at that point."

Portale tried to get Moscato to give a precise assessment of the times they arrived on Bannerman Island and that Angelika reached the island, but he could only estimate. The attorney criticized him for not writing down the hour and minute.

"I had been meeting with her for ten days. I never wrote down any of those times either that I met with her," Moscato argued.

"You're not suggesting that she confessed to murder any of those other times?"

"I didn't say that."

"But this time was a little different, right? This time—"

Moscato didn't let Portale finish his question. "I didn't have a crystal ball and knew what was going to happen—"

"Would you answer my question?" Portale asked. In the same breath he turned to the judge and pleaded, "Your Honor?"

When the attorney got no response from Freehill, he continued, "What I'll do is, I'll ask a question and then I'll give you an opportunity to answer it. Can we do that?"

"I know how the system works," Moscato snapped.

"And I promise I am not going to interrupt. I'll try not to." Portale paused and then continued, "This time was a little bit different. It was a *lot* different than the other times you met with Miss Graswald because this time, you're saying she confessed to murder, true?"

Now it was ADA Mohl's turn to object.

"What's the basis?" Portale asked.

"Number one," she said, "it's argumentative, and what time are you talking about?"

"I don't see this as being argumentative," the judge said. "I'll agree with the other part. Sustained. Rephrase the question."

Portale forged ahead. "The Bannerman's Island meeting with Miss Graswald was different than the meeting leading up to [it] because in the Bannerman's meeting on 4/29, you're saying that she confessed to murder?"

"No."

Julie Mohl objected again and was sustained by the judge. Richard Portale withdrew his question and the judge struck the answer.

Portale changed his query. "You testified on direct that you have gone to Bannerman's Island on 4/29 and were searching for clues. That true?"

"That's right."

"So, with regard to the communication that took place between you and Miss Graswald prior to arriving on Bannerman, there were some phone calls or text messages?"

"Yes."

"You called her and she returned your call?"

"No. The opposite."

"Are you sure?"

"I'm positive."

"So, she called you first and then you returned her call?"

"She called me. I answered the phone. This was at

Gully's," Moscato said, growing irritated. "This is the part where you didn't allow me to explain."

"Just answer the question," the judge remonstrated.

"You were at Gully's?" Portale asked.

Moscato confirmed again and described the phone call he'd received from Angelika. "And later on, at the island, she showed up. We didn't tell her to go there. I didn't tell her not to go there. She had planned on going there, on her own. And when she arrived at the island, yes, it was like any other time of the nine days prior of meeting with her. I had no idea that she was gonna confess to murder when she came to that island."

Portale moved to strike for non-responsiveness and the judge refused his request. The attorney asked, "My question to you, really [is] who called who first. That's the question, who called who first?"

"Well, I answered that three times and you didn't believe me," Moscato retorted. "And I even said positive. She called me first."

"You said you walked around the island. Did you walk along the outside of the island, the shoreline?" the attorney asked.

"It's hard to walk around the shoreline on the island. I don't know if you know the layout of it, but it's kind of cliffy. We docked. We went up the steps. There are trails up there and leading up to the house that was built up there. We walked around there and then we walked down to the shoreline. But it's hard to walk around the perimeter of the island, given the terrain of it."

Then Portale brought up Angelika's arrival on the island. "So, from the time Miss Graswald disembarked the boat on Bannerman's Island, to the time she got on your police boat, either yourself—aside when she was in the bathroom—either yourself or one of your troopers were with her, right?"

"Not all the time."

"Were there other places and times she wasn't with a trooper on Bannerman?"

"The island is not a big island. So, we were there on the island. Were we holding her hand? No. Was she free to go? Absolutely."

"She was gonna go where?"

"Wherever she wanted to go."

"But it's an island," Portale snipped.

"How did she get there?" Moscato pointed out. "She got there in a boat. She could have left there the same way. She was free to go. She was not in custody. And we had no reason to keep her there. We didn't—we really didn't invite her to come out there."

"She wasn't handcuffed?"

"No. Absolutely not. In fact, even after she admitted to what she did, she still wasn't handcuffed."

"This is on the island now?"

"Yes."

"So, you testified that on the island, as you were talking to her, at some point you sat down on the trail; is that right?"

"Yes."

"And prior to that, you had allowed her to smoke a cigarette, you had allowed her to go to the bathroom?"

"Yes."

"Objection, Judge," Mohl interrupted, "as to the characterization of 'allowed.'"

Portale tried to clarify: "Did she ask you?"

"Sustained," Freehill said.

"Withdrawn," said Portale. "During those times, did [she] say, like, 'Can I go to the bathroom?' Did she ask you?"

"It was more of a statement. 'Hey, I got to go to the bathroom.' 'All right, go to the bathroom. Who's stopping you?' 'I want a cigarette.' 'Sure. Have a cigarette.' It wasn't like I gave her permission to do it, no. If she wanted to do it, she was free to do it. I don't think she was looking for my approval for that. She's a grown woman; she needs to go to the bathroom, she goes to the bathroom. It wasn't like I was stopping her from going to the bathroom. I wasn't stopping her from having a cigarette."

They talked about the friendship that had grown between Moscato and Angelika in the ten days after the incident and then went through the details of the time before Angelika went off alone with Investigator DeQuarto—mild topics, but still the tone remained contentious.

When Portale accused him and the other investigators of asking Angelika pointed questions, Moscato responded, "I wanted it in her own words. It wasn't like an interrogation thing where we're asking her questions. I wanted her to tell us so that we could better get the picture of what actually happened, so that we had a better idea of where we could concentrate our efforts in looking for Vincent Viafore's body. Remember, at that time, we still had not found Vincent Viafore. So, that was one of our main concerns as law enforcement."

"Did you just testify that it was not like an interrogation; is that what you said?"

"I don't believe it was, not on my part. Now when—"

Portale interrupted, challenging Moscato's depiction of the conversations on the island. They bantered through several questions and then Portale asked, "Do you recall asking Miss Graswald, 'Angelika, what you are holding inside of you is burning a hole. If you don't let it out, it's gonna eat away at you from the inside out.' Do you recall asking her that?"

"I may have said something to that effect, yes.'

"That's exactly what you said to her, right?"

"I don't know my exact words, but something to that effect, yes."

"Because you didn't believe what happened on the river was an accident, you thought she killed Vincent Viafore, true?"

"No," Moscato said firmly. "The reason I said that to her was because of the way she was acting on the dock. She had a hard time telling me exactly where they docked the kayaks. So, she was holding back something. Did I know at that point that she, in your words, had murdered Vincent Viafore? No, I did not know that. But, obviously, something was bothering her. And I kind of sensed that. That's why I said, 'Hey, you got to let us know what is going on.'"

"Well, no, what you said was 'what you're holding inside is burning a hole in you'; is that right?"

"Okay. If that's what I said, that's what I said. You're telling me that's what I said, right?"

Portale asked several questions about Susan McCardell approaching to check in on Angelika and then said, "At no time upon Bannerman's Island on April 29, 2015, did you ever advise Miss Graswald that she was not a suspect, true?"

"Can you just say that again, please?"

"I didn't understand that either," the judge added.

"At no time—"

"At no time. It was a double negative," Moscato commented.

"Let him say it, please," the judge said, trying to ease some of the tension in the courtroom. "Let's all just take it in and hear the question."

"Why don't we phrase it in a different way, if that will help you," Portale said.

"Thank you."

"On April 29, 2015, on Bannerman's Island, did you advise Miss Graswald that she was not a suspect?"

"I didn't tell her that she was a suspect, no."

"Did you tell her that she was not a suspect?"

"Did I say: 'You are not a suspect'?"

Portale confirmed.

"No. I don't think that subject came up. Again, I hate to harp on the last nine or ten days, but we had very similar conversations for the past nine or ten days. You know, up until the point where she started opening up to the three of us, and I decided it was best, in fairness to Angelika, to have her speak solely to one investigator, which was Investigator DeQuarto."

The defense attorney turned the questioning to Angelika's missing cell phone and beat on that topic for a while before switching back to her status as a suspect.

Moscato said, "She had the most information that we were trying to glean from her. To characterize her as a suspect, that's going too far, in my opinion, at that point."

"Was there someone else that you were focusing on?"

"No. Like you said, she was the one that was last seen with him. She had the most information that would be of interest to us in pursuing any viable leads in order for us to try to figure out where Vincent Viafore's body could have either drifted to, drowned at, or got caught up on."

"Without the statement that Miss Graswald allegedly made to Investigator DeQuarto, she wouldn't have been placed under arrest at that time, correct?"

"Objection. Calls for speculation, Your Honor," ADA Mohl said.

"Speculation?" Portale exclaimed. "He's the senior investigator."

"He can answer. Overruled," the judge answered.

Moscato responded, "As senior investigator out there making a decision, no, she would not have been immediately placed under arrest if she hadn't made the further statements to Investigator DeQuarto. However, we would have continued our investigation. But, no, she would not have been placed under arrest prior to her admissions."

"When you say 'we would have continued our investigation,' you mean of Miss Graswald?"

"No. I mean locating Vincent Viafore and trying to determine exactly what happened."

Portale then asked a long series of questions about the kayak paddles. He gave Moscato a hard time when the investigator said that he had not noticed the plug was missing from the kayak, and then battered him over semantics about the condition of the paddles.

Without warning, Portale shifted gears. "You testified that you had gone to Bannerman's on April 29, 2015, to search for clues on the island, correct?"

"That is right."

"What tools did you have with you to collect those clues, if any?"

"My eyes," Moscato retorted.

"Okay. Besides your eyes, what else did you have?"

"Tools?"

"Yeah, tools."

"None."

"No forensic tools?"

"No."

Portale asked about specific tools, naming them one by one: camera, measuring tape, rulers, notepads. Moscato said he had none of the above but knew that there was a camera since some photographs were taken. He didn't know if anyone had any of the other items.

"Well, of the three of you, none of you took notes when you were having this discussion with Miss Graswald on the trail, right?"

"No, I didn't take any notes."

"Nobody did, right?"

"Well, if that's what you're saying, nobody. I didn't take any notes."

"You were sitting on the trail?"

"Right."

"Miss Graswald was there?"

"Yes."

"She didn't have any notes, right. She wasn't taking notes, right?"

"Right."

"Investigator DeQuarto was there. He wasn't taking notes, right?"

"Right."

"Investigator DaSilva was there, and you saw him, and he wasn't taking notes, right?'

"Right."

"So as far as you know, neither yourself, DaSilva, [nor] DeQuarto had a notepad with them on Bannerman's Island?"

"That's correct. As far as I know, no one had any notes, that's right."

"Did you have any evidence bags with you?"

"No. Not me personally."

"Did DaSilva have any evidence bags with him? No?"

"I don't believe so."

"And Investigator DeQuarto didn't have any evidence bags with him?"

"I don't believe so."

At the request of the defense, the court took a five-minute break.

CHAPTER TWENTY-FOUR

When Aniello Moscato returned to the witness stand, the defense attorney assured him that he only had a few more questions. Portale first wanted to know who shot the photographs on the island, but Moscato was not certain. He then took the investigator through another explanation of the difference between the Bannerman boat and the police boat.

Portale seemed intent on making Moscato erupt in anger. He'd gotten close on several occasions, but he eventually hit gold with the evidence tags, known in state police lingo as "general 40 tags." The defense attorney feigned ignorance about the writing on those forms. He refused to accept that the word "defendant" could have been added after the case turned from a missing persons category to homicide. He insisted, despite Moscato's attempt to educate him, that the incident date on the tag proved that Angelika was a suspect on the day of Vince's death. Moscato's frustration escalated with every accusatory question.

The defense once again requested a break. When they

returned, Portale went on a different attack. "So, during the break, we saw each other in the hallway?"

"Yes."

"You were with some individuals, speaking to them. Who were those individuals?"

"I spoke to everybody. I spoke to three law students. I spoke to another attorney. I spoke to the Viafore family. I spoke to almost everyone," Moscato said defensively.

"I think you know what I'm talking about. When you and I saw each other, remember that?"

"Yeah."

"Who were you with at that time?"

"Who was I with?"

"I'm asking you."

"I was with a number of different people out there, was it the three law students?"

"At the time that you and I looked at each other, we did like a salute to each other."

"You saluted me. I don't think I saluted you back," Moscato snarked.

"I thought I saw you do it?"

"I might have winked at you."

"Careful of that," the judge warned.

"I wouldn't doubt it," Portale grumbled.

"If you knew who it was, why don't you help the investigator?" Freehill told Moscato.

"Right. Can you describe the person?" Moscato asked.

"I don't know who it was," Portale said.

"I told you, I spoke to a couple of lawyers."

"There were two females."

"Two females?"

"They were blond."

"Young?" Moscato asked.

"No, about middle age."

"Where are we going here?" the judge asked.

"I can answer it now," Moscato cut in. "That was Laura Rice. That's Vincent Viafore's sister. And if—her mother was here, Mrs. Viafore. And I was also speaking to two younger—that's why I asked you if they were younger ones—I was talking to two younger interns that are doing an internship with the DA's office. They're law students."

"Okay. Thank you. No further questions," Portale said, not visibly perturbed that he'd demonstrated his lack of concern for the victim's family members by not even recognizing them.

ADA Julie Mohl approached the witness and began redirect. First, she took Moscato through a careful explanation of how evidence tags are created. She followed that by eliciting a description of a missing person investigation and the necessary contact with family members and the last known person to have seen the missing individual.

On recross, Portale dove back into the evidence tags as if he'd not heard a word of the redirect testimony. He kept making the same point again and again as if he couldn't grasp the simple facts of the process. He repeatedly misstated Moscato's testimony and twisted his words until Moscato had had enough.

The investigator leaned forward in the witness chair. "You're wrong. You're wrong. You are absolutely wrong." His voice boomed through the courtroom, his angry tone underlining every word.

"Investigator," the judge requested, "a little bit away from the microphone."

Even after that, Portale kept reiterating accusations until Freehill interrupted.

"These questions have been asked over and over again," the judge said.

"Withdrawn. No further questions." Portale surrendered the floor, seemingly unconcerned that he had just made himself appear remarkably stupid to some observers.

Senior Investigator Aniello Moscato descended from the witness box, the unwelcome specter of possibly being recalled by the defense hanging over his head.

The day in court ended with a squabble between defense and prosecution. Attorney Chartier accused the state of withholding information that should have been provided in discovery and slammed the state police and the state with being dishonest. Julie Mohl insisted that much of the material that he had requested had already been provided and called the accusations "offensive."

Judge Freehill requested some of the materials be provided and asked for another witness to clarify the details surrounding the requisition of the boat. He then dismissed the court.

CHAPTER TWENTY-FIVE

Before the court was back in session on June 9 at 11:00 am, ADA Mohl provided the defense a copy of the interrogation video with enhanced audio, as well as two photographs.

Judge Freehill brought the court to order, but he had a hard time keeping it that way. The defense team had a litany of complaints about the materials they'd just received. Portale made an insincere expression of gratitude over the photographs, before lambasting the prosecutors for not providing them sooner. He was angrier, though, about the audio-enhanced videotape of Angelika's interrogation. He wanted the judge to force the state to explain why it had taken so long to deliver.

Mohl had issues of her own. She told the judge that the defense had refused to acknowledge receipt of items and instead threw papers from her desk and a paper clip at her. She further explained that the state planned to enter the original version of the videotape, not the enhanced version, in trial, allowing the defense plenty of time to review it beforehand. Portale fired back, saying that he'd requested those materials nearly eleven months ago and accusing ADA Mohl of being dishonest.

The squabbling continued until the judge ordered everyone, including the court reporter, into his chambers. Behind closed doors, the judge made it clear that he was troubled by the 371 inaudible words in the original tape. "Do you really think that, if we render a decision that down the road is part of an appeal, and we base that decision on a tape that was not as enhanced as a later tape, we're not going to be back doing this in a couple of years, if by chance the defendant is convicted?"

After a volley of questions from the judge and arguments from both sides, the judge decided that the video with the enhanced audio needed to be presented as evidence. He offered the defense more than a week after that day's proceedings to review the enhanced video.

After lengthy discussion about conflicts, the judge set two days to finish up the proceedings, and after lunch testimony began anew.

The state called Kevin Gardner, a trooper stationed at the Kingston barracks in Ulster County. He'd been employed with the New York State Police for nearly twenty years. For the past thirteen and one-half years, he'd been a team leader for the Troop F segment of the dive team.

On April 28, 2015, he was in the middle of conducting a two-month dive school. On that crystal-clear day, they were performing strikes on the USS *Slater,* a historic battleship up in the port of Albany. Around midday, he received a call from Senior Investigator Aniello Moscato, asking if a boat was available the following morning to transport him and a couple of other investigators to Bannerman Island, down the Hudson River. He contacted two members of his team, Trooper Lance Rell and Zone Sergeant James Whittle, to see if they could assist.

ADA Julie Mohl asked, "After making those arrangements, or while making those arrangements, did you document that request for transport in any way?"

"I did not," Gardner said. "It was just a general request to bring some members across the river. It was not involving a search or a dive operation. So, I had no need to write it down."

"Is that, generally speaking, common practice not to document something like that, where a member is requesting transport?"

"Yes. For something like that, there is no protocol to have to do up an entire report for a brief ride on a boat. If there was something more extensive where we were diving or doing a sonar search, something along those lines that was more extensive, then I would do a dive report.

"My boss was up there with us for the training, my boss in Albany. So most likely, I believe I probably told him, 'Hey, we're just putting the boat out.' That was it."

Julie Mohl turned over the witness to the defense, and attorney Jeffrey Chartier did the cross-examination. He asked Gardner first for his personal cell number and then for the name of his carrier, causing Mohl to object. The judge sustained, after arguments from the defense.

Then he attempted to get Moscato's phone number from Gardner but failed. In response to questions, Gardner told the court that he'd spoken directly to Rell and Whittle and they'd agreed to transport the trailered nineteen-foot Boston Whaler, one of three boats they had available, down to Newburgh for the crossing.

Chartier then went into a line of questioning about repairs to the boat on the day in question and gassing up the boat. Gardner did not recall any repairs made to the boat after the trip to Bannerman Island and said the fueling was done at local gas stations since the state police no longer had gas pumps at their barracks.

ADA Mohl objected. "As to the relevance of this line of questioning."

"I'm hoping that Mr. Chartier is going to make that clear in a moment," Judge Freehill said.

Chartier said, "I am," but then proceeded to quibble about how the troopers paid for the gas and badgered the witness about not filing paperwork for the use of a state-owned, taxpayer-paid boat. "What's the normal procedure for requisitioning a vessel for activity?" he asked.

Mohl objected again. "It's not relevant for this. Limited scope for a specific day and incident that defense counsel was inquiring about for another witness. We brought in this witness to clarify the issue."

"Your Honor," Chartier argued, "he testified in this instance they did not utilize paperwork. I need to know in what instances they would utilize paperwork and why they didn't do it in this case."

"Your Honor," Mohl repeated, "that's irrelevant for this hearing."

"First of all," Freehill said, "the witness told you why he didn't do it. Because he didn't think he needed to. That's the answer. If you want to find out what instances, I'll give you a little leeway."

"In what instances are you required to fill out paperwork for use of this vessel?" Chartier asked Gardner.

"Although, he answered that question already to some degree, when he said when there's diving involved or something else," the judge interrupted.

Chartier agreed and reworded the question. "A list of all instances in which paperwork would be required?"

"Diving operations, sonar operations, if we're going out to do a rescue or, you know, if I was going to go out and there was a stranded boater on the river, I would do a report on it. But for just an investigator [asking] us for transport to cross to an island, I didn't need to do one."

After that, the proceedings became farcical. Chartier asked a question. Mohl objected. The judge usually sustained. Over and over again. At last, Trooper Gardner was released from the stand.

CHAPTER TWENTY-SIX

Senior ADA David Byrne called Investigator Anthony DaSilva to the stand. DaSilva had worked for the New York State Police for eleven years and served as an investigator for the past two. On April 29, 2015, he'd accompanied Senior Investigator Moscato and Investigator DeQuarto on the boat to Bannerman Island.

"Once we arrived on the island," DaSilva said, "we began to walk around and make our way to the shoreline where we could." He was dressed in a shirt, tie, and slacks, having left his jacket in the car; the other two investigators wore jeans and T-shirts.

DaSilva identified Angelika in the courtroom and was asked to describe the initial interaction between her and the senior investigator. "When she came off the boat, she said hello and it seemed to be a warm greeting. She also said hello to Investigator DeQuarto. And they introduced me as well, since I had never met her before."

"What was her demeanor at that time?" Byrne asked.

"She seemed to be in good spirits."

"Did she express surprise at seeing the police on the island?"

"No."

"What happened next?"

"Senior Investigator Moscato advised Miss Graswald that we had come out to the island to check around the shoreline. We hadn't found anything. And he asked her if she could sort of take us through the day of the nineteenth that she had been on the island with Mr. Viafore. Walk us through where they arrived, the areas on the island that they had gone to. How the day was. How the weather was. And take us through that day and back to where they left from, and exactly where left from and when."

"Did she do so?"

"She did. She sort of had a difficult time staying on track with it."

"What do you mean by that?"

"She kept stopping when we would walk, and change the subject and talk about other things that were going on. And Senior Investigator Moscato had to work to kind of keep her on track with moving forward and re-creating the day as it were."

"You said as you walked. Can you explain, please, the area that was walked, generally speaking, from the dock to the interior of the island?"

DaSilva complied. "So, when you arrive on the island, there is a dock there. You walk to a platform, off the dock where there are a couple porta-potties. Off to the right, there is a staircase that goes up a pretty large hill. Series of stairs. There [are] actually quite a few of them, with landings in between them, before you finally arrive at the top.

"When you arrive at the top, there is a series of trails that have stone walkways and even stone retaining walls around them that go to various points on the island. We went up one particular pathway that goes by a platform that overlooks the Hudson and continues on up to a residence that is sort of at the top of the island there. But we didn't make it all the way up there, I don't believe.

"We were coming back down that trail I described near that platform. And I asked Miss Graswald who she called from the rescue boat."

"What did she say, if anything?"

"She didn't answer," DaSilva said. "Investigator DeQuarto was a couple of steps away at that point. I just walked up to him, just to inquire out loud, because, again, it wasn't my case. And I wasn't there. And this was the first time I met Miss Graswald.

"I said, 'A rescue worker saw you with the phone on the boat. Who did you call?' She said, 'I had a missed call, and I tried to call it back, but the call didn't go through.' I asked her where the phone was and she said that she didn't know."

"And what happened then, if anything?"

"I said to her, 'You know, you initially told us, us being the state police, that you had lost the phone in the water.' Investigator DeQuarto told me yesterday that a rescue worker had seen you with the phone on the boat and you told him that you were going to go home and look for the phone. Your fiancé is missing, and I would think that the cell phone that contains all of your memories of him— photographs, pictures, text messages, basically documenting your life with him—I would think that that would be something very important that you would want to find. But you don't really seem to care.' And she said, 'Where is that phone? I had it at the hospital. I think the first officer that was there has the phone.'"

Soon after that discussion, DaSilva said that he and Moscato left DeQuarto to speak alone with Angelika.

DaSilva explained that he and the senior investigator walked away and didn't see the other two for forty minutes to an hour. He then corroborated Moscato's statement about DeQuarto's description of his conversation with Angelika.

"When you had the conversation with Investigator DeQuarto, where was the defendant?" Byrne asked.

"She was back up on the platform. But as he was walking towards us I saw her in the background walking on the trail, and she was going back down toward the stairs that go back down to the docks where the boats—"

"Was she in handcuffs?"

"No."

"What happened next, where did you go?"

"She came out of the bathroom and we boarded the state police boat to go back to Gully's."

"Did the defendant ever protest getting on the boat?"

"No."

"Would you please describe the defendant's demeanor on the boat?"

"She actually seemed—she wasn't holding her stomach or breathing heavy anymore. She at one point said, 'I'm free.' She seemed to be enjoying the wind. And she was whistling."

"She actually said, 'I'm free'?" Byrne emphasized.

"Yes. It was pretty surreal, actually, on the Hudson with that going on, and the engine dying, and knowing what she had just told Investigator DeQuarto."

"Was she crying?"

"No."

"Was she in cuffs on the boat?"

"No."

After landing at Gully's twenty-five minutes after leaving the island, he said, "we got off the boat. I went in Investigator DeQuarto's car with Miss Graswald sitting in the front passenger seat. I sat in the back. And we drove back to Montgomery."

"Did the defendant say anything on the way back from Gully's Landing to the state police barracks in Montgomery?"

"Yeah. She said she felt better. And as we were getting to SP Montgomery, she said that she thought that Investigator DeQuarto was cute the first time she met him."

In response to questions, DaSilva confirmed that Angelika was not in cuffs during the drive and that she never requested the presence of counsel on the island, in the boat, or in the car.

"Do you know where, if anywhere, the defendant went once you all arrived at the barracks?"

"Yes, she was placed in an interview room."

"And did you have any contact with the defendant after that?"

"No, not until much later."

The state turned over the witness and the court had a short recess before the cross-examination began. Portale questioned DaSilva about the Spectrum Justice Report and his interactions with ADA Mohl in the past two weeks. He responded that he'd met with her three or four times and had no idea if she took any notes to document those encounters.

"When were you first assigned to this case, the Graswald case?" Portale asked

"The twenty-ninth of April was the first day I became involved, nine thirty, ten in the morning."

"How did that come about?"

"I checked in with my supervisor that day, Senior Investigator Moscato. He advised me that . . . [he] and Investigator DeQuarto were going to go out to Bannerman's Island, and he asked me if I wanted to go along."

"So, that morning, prior to Bannerman's Island, did you

get up to speed or, quote, unquote, get 'read in' on the Graswald case?"

"Yeah, they told me why they were going out there. And just working in the back room there the preceding week, I started going over bits and pieces of what was going on."

"What bits and pieces are you talking about?" Portale asked.

"That they were attempting to locate Mr. Viafore in the water. That there were boats in the water. That the dive team had not located him as of yet."

"There is more, though, right? They briefed you on more than just that, right?"

"Yes, on the twenty-ninth—" DaSilva began.

"You mind if I finish the question?" Portale snapped.

"Sorry. I thought you were done."

"So did I," Judge Freehill added.

"They briefed you on more than that, they briefed you on the fact that they were suspicious about Miss Graswald's phone, correct?"

Byrne objected, and Judge Freehill sustained.

Portale took another tact. "Did you have a team meeting that morning?"

"No."

"Who was it that you met with to get read in, to get up to speed on this case?"

"I went to the barracks that morning and met with Senior Investigator Moscato. And . . . [he] and I drove to the waterfront together."

"On Bannerman's, you asked Miss Graswald several questions about her phone and the location of her phone, right?"

"Yes."

"How did you know to ask those questions?"

"During the car ride over, Senior Investigator Moscato advised me that Investigator DeQuarto had talked to Miss

Graswald in the previous evening. But he told me that they were attempting to locate her cell phone. When we got to the waterfront, we met with Investigator DeQuarto, who reiterated to me that he had spoken with Miss Graswald the night before and she had indicated that she would check her residence for the cell phone in question."

"At any time prior to April 29, 2015, and the interaction you had with Miss Graswald on Bannerman's Island, had you listened to her nine-one-one call, yes or no?" Portale asked.

"I don't think so. I remember I did hear it at one point, but I don't believe it was till after that."

"The morning of the twenty-ninth, before you went to Bannerman's Island, are you sure you didn't listen to it with Investigator DeQuarto, when you got into the barracks?"

"I don't believe [he] was at the barracks in the morning prior to going out to Bannerman's."

After discussing in more detail the sequence of events on the island, Portale asked, "You had stated on direct that you had gone to Bannerman's that morning to check the shoreline . . . why did you want to check the shoreline?"

DaSilva repeated his previous statement about no one having checked out the island itself and explained their search. "It was a little difficult due to the topography of the island, but we did the best we could to make our way from the various trails down to the water where we could and did check the shoreline, for approximately an hour."

"And about what percentage of that shoreline would you say that you covered in that time frame?"

"I think we got pretty close to doing the whole thing."

"Did you have any prods to be able to look into the water or anything?"

"No."

"You weren't able to manipulate the shoreline in any

way, with sticks or prods to see if there was something in any location that you couldn't visualize?" Portale pressed.

"No. What I was doing was just a visual inspection."

"Did you take any photos of the shoreline that you had searched on April 29 on Bannerman's Island?"

"Yes, there were some photos."

"How many photos did you take?"

"Off the top of my head, I don't recall," DaSilva admitted.

"What did you do with those photos?"

"When the camera gets downloaded, they go on the computer."

"Did you give those photos to Miss Mohl?"

"I gave her the photos pertaining to Miss Graswald's presence on the island that day."

After interrogating DaSilva on the scuba team's search of the shoreline, Portale refocused on what the investigators had been looking to find that day. "And in your search of the shoreline, were you searching for a body you believed to be floating or submerged, did you know?"

"No, I did not know. And we were also looking for belongings that might be there, not just the—ultimately, the body—but also other things that may have washed up pertaining to Mr. Viafore. Potentially anything."

"Right. Belongings that could be submerged, correct?"

"Or floating, or had been submerged and washed up or—"

Portale cut him off, "And, at the time, did you have a working knowledge of how long it would have taken, given the water temperature and the ambient temperature, and the date, for a body to float to the surface, do you know?"

"Objection, Your Honor," Byrne said, "beyond the scope."

"Sustained."

Portale asked about his client going to the restroom

unaccompanied. "Weren't you worried about her escaping or taking off? I mean, she just confessed to murder, weren't you worried?"

"It's not that large of an area," DaSilva pointed out. He gestured around the courtroom as he described the island's layout. "The platform where those porta-potties are is maybe from this table to that wall there, and, you know, the width between where the court reporter is sitting to the desk there. There is really nowhere to go; she could either go back up the stairs or down to the docks. And there is a bench there."

"And she didn't?"

"No."

"She went to the boat?"

"Correct."

"Okay. She wasn't handcuffed at that point?"

"No."

Portale moved on to the car ride from Gully's to the barracks. "And Miss Graswald rode in the front passenger seat of Investigator DeQuarto's cruiser, correct?"

"Yes, well—"

"You were in the back seat?"

"Yes."

"It wasn't his cruiser?"

"It was an unmarked cruiser, sir. An unmarked car."

"It's his car," Portale argued.

"It's a state police vehicle."

"So, she was in the front and you were in the back?"

"Yes."

"And she wasn't cuffed?"

"No."

"Why were you in the back? Were you cuffed?" Portale quipped.

Byrne immediately objected.

The defense attorney rephrased his question. "Why were you in the back and she in the front?"

"That's how we're trained."

"Prior to sitting down on the trail, the four of you, were you present for anyone expressly advising Miss Graswald that she wasn't a suspect?"

DaSilva hesitated. "Can I just have an issue with the question?" he asked. "It seems to imply that she was a suspect."

"No. I'm just asking you if anybody told her she wasn't. Did you tell her she wasn't?"

"I don't make a habit of telling people that aren't suspects that they are suspects."

"So, the answer is no?"

"That's correct."

Portale confirmed that neither DeQuarto nor Moscato had told Angelika she was a suspect either. Then he asked whether or not DaSilva had inspected the kayaks or paddles before going to Bannerman's Island and if he'd personally carried any forensic tools to collect evidence. DaSilva answered no to both questions. When Portale asked if he'd had a camera with him, he said he had.

"And did you take notes with the notepad on your cell phone?"

"No," DaSilva responded.

"You use your cell phone to record, right?"

"Yes."

"Do you do that typically during the course of your employment?"

"I do not."

"If you want to record a conversation, what do you use? Do you have a handheld recorder or something else? In the field?"

"Generally, I don't record conversations in the field,"

DaSilva explained. "One of the other investigators I work with has a handheld recording device that, if I know I'll need it in advance, it is available to me. Or if I'm at the station, I'll use it there."

"But you don't use your phone?"

"No."

"You have—I mean you could if you wanted. If you wanted to record a conversation, you have the capability?"

The judge interrupted to say, "You can do a lot of things."

"I'm sorry," Portale said.

After a brief break requested by Portale to review his notes, he continued, "From the time you came into contact with Miss Graswald on April 29, 2015, till the time you got to Gully's, she never asked for counsel, right?"

"That's correct."

"You never advised her that she had a right to counsel, correct?"

"That's correct."

"And nor did Investigator DeQuarto or Moscato, correct?"

"Not in my presence."

Portale released the witness.

ADA Byrne started the redirect. "When you had any conversation with the defendant on April 29, 2015, what language did you speak?" he asked, trying to counter the defense's argument about Angelika's inability to understand anything but her native tongue.

"English."

"What language did she speak in response to you?"

"English."

"Did she ever express a lack of capacity to understand the language you were speaking?"

"No."

"How would you characterize the tone of the conversation?"

"At the time we settled in, it was, you know, calm. And we were attempting to sort of console her at the same time as figure out exactly what the status of her cell phone was. And, also, her possible grief and her relationship with Mr. Viafore."

"Was there any yelling?"

"No."

"So, how would you describe the tone?"

"Calm, relaxed."

Byrne released the witness and court was dismissed until June 20.

CHAPTER TWENTY-SEVEN

At 10:00 am on June 20, 2016, Detective Donald DeQuarto took the stand. Prosecutor David Byrne established his twelve-year career with the New York State Police with a three-year stint as an investigator assigned to the state police Montgomery barracks. Together they went through DeQuarto's meeting with Angelika at St. Luke's Hospital and her deposition back at the barracks.

"You said that Vincent told her to call nine-one-one, correct?"

"Correct."

"Did she say, at that time, that he had said anything else to her?"

"No. She told me that's all he said."

"And you were clear about that with her?" Byrne pressed.

"Yes," answered DeQuarto. He related the conversation they'd had about Vince capsizing in the river.

"During the oral conversation with her at the barracks on that evening, did she describe if she and Vincent Viafore had any wedding plans?" Byrne asked.

"Yeah. She said they were supposed to get married, I believe it was in August."

"Did she describe where the plans were?"

"I wasn't too clear on that. She said that they thought they were trying to plan something over in Latvia, but then there may have been talk of planning a wedding in the area on Bannerman's Island."

"And during your whole conversation with her, she was clear that she was not able to get to Vincent?"

"Yes."

"And that she was exhausted?"

"Yes."

After establishing that their conversation was in English and Angelika had had no difficulty with comprehension, Byrne asked, "You described, at some point, a supporting deposition that was secured . . . how was that done?"

"I asked her the details of what happened that night and I typed it up on a computer," DeQuarto said.

"And did you ask her anything or tell her anything with respect to her viewing the document?"

"Yeah. I asked her to read it and I asked her if she wanted anything changed on it, to let me know, and if she didn't want any changes, after she read it in its entirety, to sign it."

"Did she indicate that she understood your instructions?"

"Yes."

"Did she review it in your presence?"

"Yes."

"Did she make any changes to it?"

"No."

Byrne introduced the first exhibit, a copy of Angelika's deposition from that night, and asked the investigator if he recognized it. He said he did.

"How do you recognize it to be so?"

"It's signed by myself . . . and Angelika Graswald."

The defense rose to question DeQuarto about the document before it was officially submitted into evidence. "Did you read this start to finish? The body of this supporting deposition?"

"Yes."

"Just now?" Portale shot back.

"No, not just now."

"Okay. So, I'm just curious, how do you know that this is the supporting deposition that my client signed, besides the signatures? What's contained in here that's—"

DeQuarto interrupted, "I recognize it from being a copy of what I took that night."

"But you just testified that you didn't read it."

"I didn't read it in its entirety, but—"

Portale barged on. "So, the contents of that supporting deposition, People's One, is the same content as the deposition that you took from my client?"

"Yes."

"Okay. No objection," Portale said.

Byrne resumed his questioning. "Investigator DeQuarto, did the defendant say anything more about the rescue itself?"

"No," DeQuarto answered. "She just said that three men had pulled her out of the water after ten minutes of being in the water."

"Did she describe whether or not she had a conversation with them?"

"No."

"Did she describe whether or not she asked them to search for Vincent Viafore?"

"She had said that there was her fiancé that was in the water and they brought her back to shore."

"And did she describe whether or not she was treated?"

"Yes. She said that EMC was there."

Byrne then asked about when she left the barracks and where she went.

DeQuarto said that he had driven her to her car at Plum Point at 11:00 pm.

"What was her demeanor like at Plum Point that evening?"

"She seemed calm."

"Okay," Byrne continued, "during the time that you spoke to her on April 19: on the phone before you saw her in person at the hospital, at the hospital, at the state police barracks, and also at Plum Point, for the entirety of the time that you spoke to her, did she *ever* request the presence of counsel?"

"No."

"Did she ever indicate that she did not want to speak with you?"

"No."

"Did you make any promises, coerce her in any way, make any threats in any fashion?"

"No."

Byrne walked DeQuarto through the next few days in which he had apprised Angelika of any developments in the search for Vince. Then he moved on to cover the scheduled interviews that Angelika had accepted and missed and her belated appearance on the evening of April 28.

"What was the sum and substance of that conversation?" Byrne asked.

"I asked her to take me through the sequence of events of that day, to tell me a little bit about themselves, about Vincent, and she stated, in sum and substance, that they were together for about a year and seven months."

DeQuarto repeated the description of the accident Angelika had given him at their meeting. "They were heading back around seven-oh-two and she knew that that was pretty much the exact time they were leaving because she had sent a text message to one of the volunteers that worked on Bannerman's Island at that time. And she said that Vincent had tipped over in his kayak because of the rough waters and reiterated, pretty much, what she told me on the first night. And she was breathing heavy."

Byrne repeated the questions he'd asked earlier, getting DeQuarto to once again assert that he'd communicated with Angelika in English and did not coerce her, threaten her, or make any promises. The only distinction in this series was a question about her demeanor on April 28. "She was holding her stomach and breathing heavy," DeQuarto said.

The prosecutor asked, "During your conversation with her, did she indicate that she lost anything else in the water, besides her phone? Did she talk about a wallet or anything else?"

"Yes, she had a wallet that, I believe, had some credit cards and her license in [it]."

Byrne moved back to the central incident. "Did she describe in more detail what happened to Vincent out on the water?"

"She said that he was in the water and he was holding on to a blue flotation device and his kayak and he also had, I believe it was a dry bag with some belongings in it, and he had asked her to call nine-one-one. She said she called nine-one-one and then when she got rescued, she said she couldn't see him anymore at that point."

"When she still could see him, according to her, was she describing what she could see of his body in the water?" Byrne asked.

"She said she saw his head just bobbing up and down."

"Did she describe the conditions, the weather conditions, on the way from Plum Point to Bannerman's Island?"

"She said the water was choppy, but it got progressively worse as they were at the island."

"Did you ask her then, 'Well, why didn't you leave earlier?'"

"Yeah," the investigator said. "She said because they were having a good time."

"During your conversation with her on the twenty-eighth, was she ever in cuffs?"

"No."

"Was she ever told she was under arrest?"

"No."

"And also, going back to your conversation on Sunday, April 19, was she ever in handcuffs?"

"No."

Byrne took DeQuarto step by step through April 29 and the time he spent with Angelika out on the island, when she'd first mentioned the plug. "Are you a kayaker?" he asked.

"No, I'm not."

"At that time, was any plug recovered in the investigation?"

"No."

"Was any ring recovered in the investigation?"

"No."

"So, when the defendant spoke those words, were you seeking clarification from her as to what she was talking about?"

"I had never kayaked a day in my life and I don't really know the importance of any kind of ring on a paddle. I didn't even know paddles have rings on them, safety rings, or in particular, that kayaks have plugs, so, she was telling me this, I really wasn't sure, and I needed to clarify what she was saying because, like I said, I never kayaked, ever."

ADA Byrne once again established that Angelika never asked for counsel, was not coerced in any way, was never in handcuffs, and had displayed no difficulty in comprehending or speaking English. Then he introduced three photographs: of the dock, the decking area, and the trail that Angelika and DeQuarto had followed.

Defense attorney Portale spoke up, badgering the witness about who'd taken the photographs, when they were taken, and if they really did represent the area as it was when he was there. After all that, he did not object to the submission of the exhibits.

The prosecutor then asked a series of questions about the areas depicted in the pictures and asked, "About how much time did you speak with the defendant without Investigator DaSilva or Senior Investigator Moscato?"

"I would say it was approximately an hour."

DeQuarto then described their return to Gully's and the car ride to the state police barracks in Montgomery. He stated that he did not ask any questions of Angelika prior to their arrival at the barracks.

"Did there come a time when you advised her of what's commonly known as Miranda warnings?" Byrne asked.

"Yes."

"How was that done?"

"In writing, a piece of paper that is a photocopy of a Miranda card."

The prosecutor offered a copy of the Miranda card as evidence. Portale jumped at this. "This is a copy of your card?" he asked DeQuarto.

"That's correct."

"So, where is your card now?"

"In my vehicle."

"Is that where you keep it commonly?"

"Yeah."

"You don't keep it on your person?"

"No," the investigator said.

Portale asked, "Did you read from this copy, or was it some other copy?"

"I don't know if it was that copy, but that's a copy of my card."

The defense dropped any objections to entering the warning into evidence, and DeQuarto read the Miranda statement aloud for the record.

Byrne continued his questioning. "During the course of the interview, from roughly three twenty or so pm on Wednesday, April 29, to roughly two thirty four am on April 30, 2015, were any breaks taken?"

"Angelika had several bathroom breaks," DeQuarto said. "I personally gave her some water crackers, pizza, cigarettes, and I know that I made her some tea. Other members that were working that night made her coffee, and someone went out and they got tampons as well."

"For approximately how long of that time period was the defendant alone in the interview room?"

"I would say about six hours," DeQuarto estimated.

"At times when the defendant was alone in the interview room what did you see, if anything, her doing?"

"She was drawing at one point, writing on paper that was in the room. At other times she was stretching and doing yoga."

The defense quibbled about the investigator's ability to testify that the complete eleven-hour tape was a fair and accurate reflection of the defendant's time in the room, since he sometimes was not present. He also pressed the witness regarding who'd copied the recording to a DVD, who'd applied noise reduction to the tape, and when he had last viewed the DVD. DeQuarto had no precise answers for any of the queries.

That series of questions incited an argument between the prosecution and the defense. "He has to have seen and heard everything that happened during that interview in order to actually be able to say that this disk is a fair and accurate depiction of what happened," Portale insisted.

"That's incorrect," Byrne argued.

"If the witness wasn't there for half an hour, let's say he went out to get pizza, which we know he did, then he can't say that what's on this disk is actually what happened, because he wasn't there—"

"He said it's a fair and accurate recording. He is familiar with the system," Byrne objected.

The two attorneys bickered back and forth for a few minutes, gaining no ground on either side. "So, we're back in the 'Twilight Zone' again," Portale cracked. "He could have watched it a hundred times. If he wasn't there and didn't see it or hear it, he doesn't know if that's accurate."

Finally, the judge ordered Portale to move on. The defense attorney went to question the timing and frequency of DeQuarto's breaks from the interview room. Again, the detective could not answer because he hadn't kept track.

The state submitted another evidentiary exhibit: the paper Angelika had drawn on. One drawing, made at De-Quarto's request, depicted one beer each in the kayaks—a Modelo for Angelika and a Dos Equis for Vince. The judge admitted it into evidence over the defense's objections.

Byrne presented the document to Investigator De-Quarto. "Indicating the bottom of that document, is there a word there?"

"Yes. . . . 'Free.'"

"And is there a drawing there?"

"Yes, it's a picture of an island, of a palm tree, some water surrounding the island, and a picture of a sun with some birds."

Byrne then pointed to the Miranda warning near the top of the paper and DeQuarto acknowledged that it was written in English.

"And a drawing of two kayaks with paddles, correct?"

"That's correct."

Then Byrne drew his attention to a symbol at the top.

"It looks like the shape of a heart," DeQuarto said.

CHAPTER TWENTY-EIGHT

After a lunch break, the hearing continued with the introduction of defense exhibits A through W, many of which were DeQuarto's investigatory notes. Then DeQuarto was back on the stand for cross-examination.

The defense first asked the detective if he had testified in court about this case prior to today. DeQuarto testified that he had not. Portale then presented the exhibits, including the report about the conversation with Angelika on Bannerman Island the investigator had typed out, signed, and dated "April 30th, 2015," as well as the notes he'd used to compile the report.

DeQuarto told the court he had written down the notes on April 30 and Portale questioned the accuracy of his statement several times as if he didn't believe him—or didn't want the judge to find him credible. Next, he queried the witness about the kayak and paddles, establishing that DeQuarto did not personally recover them, although he had signed off on their transfer to the Storm King Fire Department.

"You had testified on direct that you had taken Miss

Graswald back to the Jeep—Mr. Viafore's Jeep—on the nineteenth; is that right?" Portale asked. "And then she was allowed to go back home, or wherever she had gone in the Jeep, with those keys that she had?"

"Correct."

Byrne rose to his feet. "Objection, Your Honor, to the word 'allowed,' as opposed to what she did."

"You didn't stop her, did you?" Portale asked.

"You can answer that part that way," the judge told DeQuarto.

"No, I did not stop her," he answered.

"So, you gave her a ride from the barracks to the Jeep and she went wherever she was going?" Portale continued.

"Correct."

Portale handed over defendant's exhibit W and asked, "What is that form?"

DeQuarto scanned the document. "It is a property receipt."

"And it is a property receipt for two silver keys . . . are those the Jeep keys that Miss Graswald had at the time, or are those some other keys?"

"I didn't fill this form out, so I'm not sure."

"I mean, you're the lead investigator in this case, right?" Portale asked, sarcasm dripping off every word.

"Yes, I am."

"Okay. So, on that night, you didn't recover the keys from her, you gave them back to her? Did you take the keys from her?"

After an objection from the state, DeQuarto responded, "As I stated, I did not fill this form out or issue this property receipt—so I don't know."

The defense attorney moved on to grilling DeQuarto about his meetings with ADA Mohl and ADA Byrne, inquiring how many times they'd met and if the attorneys had taken notes. He asked if DeQuarto or his colleagues

Moscato and DaSilva had discussed their testimony with other witnesses, and DeQuarto said no. Portale brought in four defense exhibits of DeQuarto's notes, asking where and when they were written. DeQuarto said that the notes were taken on April 27 at the barracks.

"You didn't take those notes at the hospital with my client?"

"No."

"When you arrived at St. Luke's Hospital on 4/19, was Miss Graswald in her hospital bed?"

"She was getting changed, I believe. The curtain was closed."

"Could you see in . . . through the curtain?" the defense attorney said, implying inappropriate behavior.

"No." DeQuarto was adamant.

"So how do you know she was getting changed?"

"I spoke to Trooper Freeman and asked how she was, and he said she was in there, getting changed."

Portale then wanted to know why the investigator took Angelika back to the barracks for further discussion.

"Because that's what we do," DeQuarto shot back.

"Well, you could have had her fill out a statement and take notes at the hospital, right?"

"I don't carry that type of paperwork—I was at the hospital. So, for me to bring her back to the station where I have my computer, where I can type up the form, was better."

DeQuarto's attention was then directed to people's exhibit 1. "What's the name of that form—the New York State form?" Portale asked.

"General Four."

"That's a criminal supporting deposition, correct?"

"I just know it as a supporting deposition."

Byrne, who was willing to butt heads with opposing

counsel as much as ADA Mohl was, said, "Objection, Your Honor."

"Criminal cases?" Portale clarified.

"Asked and answered and also beyond the scope of this hearing," Byrne said.

The judge sustained the objection and Portale forged ahead. "Did you take any handwritten notes with regard to what you entered into the supporting deposition?"

"No."

"You typed it as you went?"

"Yes."

"Why was it important to have Miss Graswald sign anything in that date and time and place?"

"Objection, Your Honor. There was no testimony that it was important to do that," Byrne said.

"Was it?" Portale asked.

"The objection is sustained," the judge said. "Don't answer that question. You can rephrase," he told DeQuarto.

Portale tried again. "Was it important to you to have her sign the supporting deposition at that date, time, and place?"

Again, ADA Byrne objected. "The detective's belief of whether it was important or not important does not resolve—"

"Sustained," the judge ordered.

Portale argued with the judge, citing cases against his decision.

"Your Honor," Byrne said, "what's controlling is the court of appeals standard, *People versus Yukl,* which is what an innocent person, in the defendant's position, would believe, with respect to custody. The subjective belief of the officers, subjective belief of the defendant, is not controlling."

"The objection is sustained again," Freehill agreed.

Portale continued, "You could have allowed Miss Graswald to go home, get a good night's sleep, and take her deposition in the morning, correct?"

Byrne lodged another objection. "It calls for speculation, and asked what he could have done, as opposed to what actually happened."

"Sustained."

Portale then confirmed that the conversation with Angelika at the barracks on April 28 had lasted from half an hour to forty-five minutes and that DeQuarto had learned that she was a beneficiary of Vince's life insurance policy a few days after the incident. The detective also affirmed that he had asked Angelika about her cell phone, her relationship with Vince, the evening before the accident, and the event itself.

"Prior to the twenty-eighth, did you take a ride on a boat with Miss Graswald to try to ascertain the location of where Mr. Viafore had gone into the water?" Portale asked.

"I did not."

"Do you know if any members of the New York State Police had done that?"

"I don't know."

Portale shifted gears. "Let's go back to the meeting of the twenty-eighth. Did you arrange that meeting with Miss Graswald, or was there assistance from Laura Rice or someone else?"

"She showed up at the barracks with Laura Rice, yes."

"Had you spoken to Miss Rice about trying to have Miss Graswald meet you at the barracks?"

"I did speak to her, yes."

"Was that on the twenty-sixth, the twenty-seventh, or some other date?"

"I spoke with Angelika on the twenty-sixth. So, it was either the twenty-sixth or the twenty-seventh. I don't recall which day it was."

"Why did you go to Bannerman's Island on 4/29?"

"Objection, Your Honor, for the purposes of this hearing, it is not relevant," Byrne cut in.

"Well, it was part of his direct testimony," Portale retorted, "as to why he went to the island to walk the shoreline to look for the body."

"You can answer," the judge told DeQuarto. "Overruled."

"Why did you go to Bannerman's Island on 4/29/15?"

"To do a search of the island and the shoreline."

"What were you looking for?"

"Anything that might assist us in locating Vincent Viafore."

"Did you personally walk the shoreline?"

"I did."

After another round of time-wasting questions and objections over DeQuarto's work schedule, Portale returned to the April 28 meeting. "The conversation you had with my client, she informed you that she was going to the Cornwall Yacht Club the next morning because she was going to float some flowers, is that right? In the honor of Mr. Viafore?"

"Yes."

"And that she was going to be floating them from Bannerman's?"

"She didn't mention Bannerman's Island. She told me she would be going to the Cornwall Yacht Club."

"What time did you arrive on Bannerman's Island on April 29, 2015?"

"It was approximately eleven am."

"Did you have your badge and your gun with you?"

"I carry my wallet, which has my shield in it, but I don't believe I had my gun with me."

Portale expressed surprise he didn't have his weapon and that he didn't bring any material for evidence collection. He also questioned the witness about the lack of equipment brought over by the scuba team. "Prior to April 29, 2015, that scuba team did not do a submerged scuba search of the shoreline of Bannerman's Island, correct?"

After objections from the state that the judge sustained, Portale changed the topic. "What time did you encounter Miss Graswald?"

"I think it was a little bit after twelve pm, twelve fifteen maybe."

"Where exactly was she when you first observed her on Bannerman's?"

"She was coming in on a boat."

"She had a life preserver with the flowers?"

"I didn't see her with it, no."

Portale badgered the detective for assuming Angelika had brought the wreath to the island, even though he hadn't seen her carry it. He did see it on the dock but did not see it in her hand, DeQuarto said.

Portale presented him with a photograph of the dock in the state exhibits, but the investigator insisted that the shot did not include the area of the dock where the wreath had rested on a wooden box.

"While you were on Bannerman's Island with Miss Graswald, did you ever ask her to stand on the shore and show you the line that they took when they left Bannerman's?"

"I don't recall that."

"While you were talking and talking to Miss Graswald on Bannerman's Island on April twenty-ninth, at some point she began to breathe heavily and she began to hold her stomach; is that right?"

"That's right."

"You had testified on direct that you had questioned her about her honesty, correct?"

"That's correct."

"But this Investigator DaSilva was also questioning her about her honesty, right?"

"Yes."

"As was Investigator Moscato? All three of you were questioning her on it, yes?"

DeQuarto replied, "I don't recall Investigator Moscato questioning her honesty. I remember him saying, you know, 'Whatever you're holding inside of you is burning a hole in you.'"

After a short recess, Portale and DeQuarto battled over semantics: whether Angelika had been "upset" or "very upset" while she was being questioned by the state police detectives. The squabble involved finding and providing DeQuarto with the report he'd filed that contained the word "very."

With that resolved, another skirmish erupted when Portale asked, "At that point, Miss Graswald was the focus of your investigation?"

The judge overruled an objection from the state and Portale continued.

"So, as you sat down and you questioned Miss Graswald, right, about lying and the truth, she was the focus of your investigation?"

"That's not correct," DeQuarto said.

"Well, you noted in your notes that prior to 4/29 you thought it was suspicious that she did not show much emotion for somebody who apparently was watching her fiancé disappear, correct?"

"That's correct."

"You also were suspicious of the fact that she had posted photos and videos of herself on social media, correct?"

"I was not suspicious of her," DeQuarto argued. "I thought that the actions I observed were odd and could be considered out of character."

"Out of character for whom?"

"For someone who is grieving."

Portale questioned the detective about his note that Angelika hadn't appeared to make Vince's disappearance her primary priority before April 29. Then he asked, "You're saying that she was not the focus of the investigation, but I'm trying to understand, what were you asking her about, what were you questioning her about, what were you trying to find out?"

"Well, you know, Angelika was the last person that was with Vincent Viafore, and she knew the most about him. So, I was trying to find out as many details as possible about them, about their relationship, anything that could provide us with a timeline to set up, because she was the last person that was with him, and we still [had] not located Vincent Viafore at this time."

"Well, is it your testimony that you were trying to locate Mr. Viafore's body and that's why you were asking these questions?" Portale pressed.

"My focus of the investigation was to find Mr. Viafore, and if there were some inconsistencies that I noted, or some behavior that I thought might have been odd, and I was speaking to her about it, it was to clarify the inconsistencies."

"You asked her how long she had been in this country, correct?"

"I believe I may have. I don't recall if it was exactly that."

"How did asking her how long she had been in this country, how was that going to help you locate Mr. Viafore's body?"

"I asked her numerous questions," DeQuarto countered. "I asked her about Vincent's vehicle, if it was paid off . . . in an investigation like this, where somebody is missing, there can never be enough information that's provided."

"My question to you is: How did asking her when she

came to this country, how was that going to help you locate Mr. Viafore's body?"

"It probably wasn't," the investigator admitted.

Judge Freehill interrupted, "What does that have to do with the voluntariness of her statements?"

"It has to do with whether she was the focus of the investigation, because they were investigating her, not the location of the body. May I continue?" Portale asked the judge.

"Objection, Your Honor," Byrne said. "Defense counsel just made a statement to Your Honor which really should be made before a jury in closing arguments, so—"

"No," Portale said.

"It seems to be a fine line between that. I agree, Mr. Byrne," the judge said. He turned to Portale. "Continue."

"Going back to whether or not Miss Graswald was the focus of your investigation on 4/29, when you asked her on Bannerman's Island, you knew she was the beneficiary of Mr. Viafore's life insurance policies, correct?"

"That's correct."

"And you had listened to the nine-one-one tape that morning and you became suspicious of her after listening to that nine-one-one tape?"

"That's not correct," DeQuarto said.

"Well, didn't you write in your report that you listened to the nine-one-one tape on the morning of the twenty-ninth and you became suspicious of her?"

"No, I did not write that I became suspicious of her. I said that in the nine-one-one call she didn't appear to be out of breath."

After several objections and the judge's rulings, Portale moved on to the moment when Investigator Moscato had asked Angelika if she wanted to speak to one person alone.

"Now, at that point, did you go somewhere with Miss Graswald alone or did they leave?"

"They left."

"They left you sitting there?"

"Correct."

"At that point, did you advise Miss Graswald of her constitutional right to remain silent?" Portale asked.

"No."

"Did you advise her that she had the right to an attorney?"

"No."

"At this point, did you remind her of her Miranda Rights?"

"No."

"And you know the Miranda Rights, yes?"

"Of course."

The defense fell into a rut of serial repetition, the state fired one objection after another, and the judge sustained each one. Finally, Freehill called it a day, recessing the court until the next morning.

CHAPTER TWENTY-NINE

The Huntley Hearing had emotionally exhausted Vince's family members as if it were the trial itself. Now, on the final day, they fervently hoped this step would be completed within hours, but they'd grown accustomed to delays that dragged the process on and on. They were filled with anxiety that this would happen yet again and make their never-ending quest for justice a journey that would never reach its destination.

Richard Portale began the morning by handing the judge copies of Court of Appeals case law, in an attempt to block the introduction of Angelika's taped interrogation at trial. Prosecutor Byrne contended that the same case law proved that all the state needed to submit was a witness to authenticate the recording, and argued that their witnesses had done just that. The judge ended the discussion by saying he would allow both sides to submit any additional arguments or materials on the issue.

With that temporarily settled, Investigator Donald DeQuarto returned to the stand to continue his cross-examination by Portale.

"You testified that, on Bannerman's Island April 29, 2015, when you were seated on the trail—yourself, Investigators Moscato and DaSilva, and my client—that a volunteer had come up to speak with Miss Graswald; is that correct?"

"Yes."

"And how many times did that volunteer come up to speak with Miss Graswald at that time?"

"One time."

"Had there been other times that that volunteer had come up?"

"Yes," DeQuarto conceded.

"How many other times?"

"One other time."

"One other time?"

"Once on the trail and once on the—"

"So, two, total?" Portale interrupted.

"Yes."

"Are you sure?"

"Yes."

Byrne objected. "Asked and answered from yesterday and asked and answered from today."

"It seems that way, Mr. Portale," the judge said. "If you have something that differs, just proceed on that."

Portale moved on. "What was the name of the volunteer?"

"I believe her first name was Susan."

"Did you speak to her on the island?"

"No."

"Did you speak to her at some point afterward?"

"Yes."

"Do you know her last name?"

"McCardell."

"Where did you speak to her after that?"

"Objection, Your Honor," Byrne cut in again. "No relevance to this proceeding whatsoever as to the voluntariness of the defendant's statements."

"Really?" Portale asked. "Because this woman, he's saying, came over to check on Miss Graswald to see if she's okay, so that's actually pretty relevant."

"What happened to her is already on the record," Byrne argued.

"What was her demeanor, what was her mind-set?" Portale countered.

Judge Freehill asked, "So, are you calling her to see if she thought Miss Graswald was in custody?"

"If I may," Portale answered, "we have observations from three New York State Police officers, those are the actual guys doing the interrogating, so, yeah, we actually are entitled to call Ms. McCardell, if we can find her, to testify as a witness. Defense cannot call witnesses that can testify to their observations? Only the government is allowed to call witnesses, is that what we are going to do?"

The situation devolved into a bitter argument, leading the judge to ask the clerk to read the initial question back to the court. Upon hearing it again, the judge ruled that it could be answered. DeQuarto said that he spoke to Susan later at the state police barracks.

"You had a conversation with Investigators DaSilva and Moscato after speaking to Miss Graswald alone on Bannerman's Island, correct?" the defense attorney asked.

"Correct."

"And you had related to them what you thought Miss Graswald said to you?"

"Objection, Your Honor," the state interrupted. "Asked and answered."

"This is all repetitive," the judge agreed.

"No, it's not. I want to know—" Portale began

"It's a recap," the judge insisted. "You're going back and asking."

"It's foundation, I want to know what it is they said to him. It's fair play; they're saying that she just confessed to murder. Their reactions to that is absolutely fair play. Was she placed in handcuffs?"

After further back-and-forth between the prosecutor and defense lawyer, the judge sustained the state's objections, chastising the lawyers for arguing over each other.

Portale tried a different tack. "When you were on Bannerman's, did you ask any of the volunteers that were there whether they had recovered anything that might relate to Miss Graswald's case?"

"No," DeQuarto said.

"You testified, I think on direct, that the volunteers were there as a cleanup crew?"

"There were volunteers there, yes."

Portale then showed the investigator four photographs and asked if they were the ones he had taken of the kayaks and the paddles. DeQuarto insisted that they were not the ones he'd testified to taking with the station camera. The photographs he'd taken were burned to a DVD, he said, and eventually given to Ms. Mohl.

Portale, however, kept asking him about the pictures as if DeQuarto had given the opposite response. The judge interrupted and asked the witness, "Did I miss something? Did you say these aren't them?"

"These are not the photos."

Portale continued his questioning, implying that the investigator didn't know which kayak belonged to whom. DeQuarto asserted that he'd learned that information from Angelika's deposition on April 19, 2015.

The defense attorney switched to another topic, trying to insinuate an inappropriate friendship between DeQuarto and Angelika. "You had testified on direct that Miss Graswald had told you that she thought you were cute?"

"Yes."

"Did you write that in any of your reports?"

"I don't believe so."

"In fact, you have two pages of handwritten notes from that day, from the twenty-ninth, right?"

"Yes."

"You have several other handwritten notes that we went over yesterday; do you remember those?"

"Yes."

"How many pages was your New York State Police incident report?"

"I don't recall at the moment."

"Let's look at it," he said, picking it up from the defense table and flipping through it. "Thirteen pages. And nowhere in that report did you write that Miss Graswald told you she thought you were cute, right?"

"No," DeQuarto admitted.

"You testified also on direct that Miss Graswald had offered to give you some gift cards and some figurines; do you remember that testimony?"

"Yes."

"That's not contained anywhere in any of your reports, is it, either of those two gestures?"

"I don't believe so, no."

"All right, let's talk a little bit about this videotaped question and answer with Miss Graswald. The entire length of that interrogation video, according to your direct testimony, is eleven hours and ten minutes. Is it fair to say that, the last hour or so, there's no real conversation going on, it's just Miss Graswald by herself in the room?"

"I believe she was in there and she was taken out for processing at one point."

"But the last hour is not much interaction, not much question and answer?"

"No."

"And you testified that Miss Graswald was alone for six hours of the eleven; is that what you said on direct?"

"Yes."

"Well, I mean, she was given eight breaks, correct?"

"I don't recall the number of breaks."

"All right. So, if we played the different breaks on the video, would that help you remember?"

"Objection, Your Honor," Byrne interrupted. "Your Honor ruled yesterday that defense counsel could use the video for purposes of impeachment—"

Portale walked back his comment. "Let's go back to—"

Byrne interrupted him in turn, asserting that the videotape had already been submitted as evidence and it spoke for itself, so any testimony about its contents was redundant. Portale argued that the state was expecting a piece of evidence to authenticate itself.

Judge Freehill intervened. "Well, in this particular case, we're not going to do it. Obviously when I look at the full tape, I'm going to see how many breaks the defendant had."

Portale forged ahead. "Investigator Skarkas was alone with Miss Graswald without you present seven different times, correct?"

"I don't know how many times," DeQuarto said.

"You don't know, or you don't remember?"

"I don't recall how many times," he clarified.

"Well, I have some questions about some of the questions that were asked and the answers that were given between Investigator Skarkas and Miss Graswald, so, are you going to be able to testify about those?"

Another objection from ADA Byrne. "The content of what Miss Graswald said is not relevant to this proceeding in the context of the video interview. It doesn't matter whether you admitted or denied, just that her statements were voluntary. She could have said nothing all that time. She could have said 'I did it,' 'I didn't do it.' Who cares when the only relevant issue is voluntariness? The only question is, did she say what she said voluntarily."

After another exchange between the lawyers, the judge dismissed court for its lunch recess.

Investigator DeQuarto returned to the stand after lunch and Richard Portale continued in his combative style. He pressed the witness for the detailed timing of his whereabouts during the first three hours of the interrogation and tried to depict the investigator as callously ignoring Angelika's emotional state.

"During those initial three-plus hours, you're with Miss Graswald, she indicates to you on four different occasions that she's tired, correct?"

"I don't recall."

"Five different times during that initial period, she asked you questions and indicates to you that she is on her period; do you remember that?"

"Yes."

"And then, again, about somewhere between five and six hours, then she brings it up again; do you remember that?"

"I do not remember her bringing it up again."

"Four times during that three-or-plus-hour period when you are with her, she's crying, correct?"

"I didn't count the number of times, so I can't answer that really," DeQuarto said.

"Do you remember, do you want to try to remember?"

"I recall her crying to a point. I don't recall how many times she was crying."

"In fact, on twelve different occasions in the first six hours, you personally accused her of either lying or not being truthful or not being honest, correct?"

"Again, I didn't count the times."

"Do you want to try to count them now?" Portale asked.

"I won't be able to remember that now."

"During the entire eleven-plus hours, she's breathing heavily, yes, holding her stomach?"

"Not for the duration of eleven hours, no."

"For the majority of the eleven hours she is?"

"There are times in the video she is, yes."

"About two hours in, you allow her to use the bathroom?"

"Somewhere around there."

Then Portale, who'd just questioned the detective about his client being on her menstrual cycle at the time of the interview, brought up Angelika's own contradiction. "And she comes back and relates to you that she thought she maybe had a miscarriage; do you remember that?"

"Yes," DeQuarto said, but didn't elaborate or mention his offer to get her medical help.

"So those first three hours, she doesn't admit to you that she has killed Mr. Viafore, correct?"

"Again, I can't recall or remember the entirety of the duration on the video because it's been memorialized on DVD and it's a very lengthy video, so for me to recall specific times during that, I don't think it's possible," DeQuarto argued.

"Prior to Investigator Skarkas reentering the room for the first time, she had admitted to killing Mr. Viafore?"

The state objected to the question and the judge sustained it.

Portale tried again. "So, prior to Investigator Skarkas reentering the room for the first time, did Miss Graswald admit to killing Mr. Vincent Viafore?"

Byrne objected. "The basis being whether she admitted it or denied it is irrelevant. The only issue is [if] what she said was said voluntarily."

"I'm going to give a little bit of leeway," the judge said. "I agree with Mr. Byrne, but this is going to some direction that is going to involve the issue of voluntariness. I'll let it go."

The question was read back and DeQuarto answered, "I'm not sure at what point that she says that she intentionally removed a plug from his kayak so that he would drown."

Portale then went through a series of queries about what was said and when while DeQuarto was absent from the interrogation room, in an attempt to prove the investigator could not authenticate the video since he was not there the entire time.

DeQuarto reiterated, "As I stated earlier, it would be impossible for me to remember a six-hour interview word for word. So, I would have to review it to refresh my recollection."

"Do you recall at 4:46:38 of the interrogation video, Investigator Skarkas is alone with my client and he tells her that this is her window of opportunity? He says, 'This is for you to provide what I call, you know what I mean, your slice of the pie, your version of the truth from your perspective. There's only one person in the world that can provide that perspective and that's you, you know what I mean. You don't want other people or other things to portray a picture of you that's going to be unfair. And, obviously, the facts are what the facts are.' Do you remember that?"

"I remember something of that context, yes."

"And then at 5:18:36, yourself and Investigator Skarkas are together with Miss Graswald and Investigator Skarkas says, 'You don't want anyone to have your slice of the pie. You want to keep those walls and keep up those barriers and not open up to us, you let other people tell your version of the truth and have your slice of pie'; do you recall that?"

"Yes," DeQuarto said.

"So, about seven hours in, at 7:03:43 time stamp, Investigator Skarkas is alone with Miss Graswald and do you remember her asking him about Miranda?"

"No."

"Were you there when that happened?"

"No."

'Were you watching through the two-way mirror, listening?"

"I never watched through the two-way mirror."

'You didn't?" Portale seemed surprised.

"No."

"So, you have no knowledge of my client asking, 'What's Miranda?,' 'Who's Miranda?,' seven hours in?" Portale said, insinuating that these questions meant that Angelika didn't understand the warning. He failed to mention the context that implied she was merely inquiring about the historical basis for the name.

"As I stated earlier, I cannot remember every single thing that happened in that video. I've reviewed it. I've been in and out of the room while Investigator Skarkas was speaking with your client, but I cannot remember every word or conversation that occurred between them."

"Well, this isn't a matter of remembering. You weren't there for it and you didn't hear it when it happened, right?"

"No."

"You administered my client's Miranda warnings. You read it to her from a card. Are you sure she understood what you were saying?"

"Yes, I am."

"Well, but later on she says, 'Who's Miranda?, 'What's Miranda?'; how do you know she understood?"

"I asked her if she understood and she said yes," DeQuarto argued.

"Are you aware that as she sat in that room, she read from her piece of paper and you could hear it on video, are you aware of this? 'You have the right to talk to a lawyer or to have one present while you're being questioned'; she was questioning that. Did you hear that?"

Byrne objected, and the judge overruled.

"I remember her reading the piece of paper and writing it on to a piece of paper, the Miranda warnings," DeQuarto said.

"At any point during this eleven-plus hours, did you read her Miranda warnings again to her?"

"No."

"Did Investigator Skarkas come up to you and say, 'Hey, listen, she's questioning Miranda,' did you have a conversation with him about that?"

"No."

"Did Investigator Skarkas reread Miss Graswald her Miranda warnings at any point?"

"Not that I'm aware."

"Well, it's yes or no. You've authenticated the video. So, did he do it or didn't he do it?"

"No."

When Portale again tried to argue that DeQuarto couldn't authenticate the video because he couldn't recall what had happened while Skarkas was alone in the room with Angelika, ADA Byrne stepped in to object.

"It's the test of witness recall based upon an interview which is reflected in an exhibit before this court, that's what this is, as opposed to testing the truth, which is reflected in the video before this court. It's a testing of the witness's recall of an eleven-hour incident."

"I don't even understand what that means," Portale said. "But the bottom line is it—"

Judge Freehill cut him off. "That's another version of saying the video speaks for itself."

"And I'm also questioning my position of authentication," Portale continued. "It's impossible for him to authenticate this video. I just wanted—"

The judge interrupted the defense again. "I doubt if it's going to come out exactly the way you want it, but that objection is sustained and you can continue questioning."

Forced to move on, Portale asked, "Do you recall Miss Graswald's demeanor when she was being interviewed by Investigator Skarkas?"

"No."

Portale then asked a series of questions about jumps or skips in the video, where DeQuarto had reviewed the video, whether it was the original or enhanced version, where he'd gotten it from, and where and when he had watched it.

When DeQuarto said that he watched it on his computer in the barracks, Portale said, "You didn't put it back into the same machine that recorded it?"

"No."

"Did you sit for eleven hours?"

"On and off, yes . . . I took a break. I didn't sit there for the duration of the video, but I viewed the whole video in a single day."

Circling back to the events on April 29, Portale asked, "So, at the conclusion of the video and after Miss Graswald was processed, what did you do?"

"I was hanging out at the barracks, speaking to investigators."

"Who did you speak to?"

"Objection, Your Honor," Byrne said, "relevancy for this hearing."

Portale withdrew the question and the judge said, "Good."

Portale continued, "At some point, you took down some notes about your conversation at Bannerman's, right?"

"Correct."

"When was that?"

"About three in the morning."

"After that eleven-plus hours you spent with my client, you went back and wrote notes from your memory about your conversations on Bannerman's, yes?"

"That is correct."

With that, Portale handed the witness back to the prosecution team. The state had no additional questions and, with that, the prosecution rested their case. In the courtroom, Vince's family breathed a sigh of relief. They were one step closer to this ordeal being over.

CHAPTER THIRTY

After a brief recess, the defense called their first and only witness to the stand. Susan McCardell, the mother of three grown sons, worked as a bookkeeper in Redding, Connecticut. She graduated from Purdue University in Indiana with a bachelor's degree in math education and earned her MBA at Pace University in New York. In her spare time, she loved to garden and volunteered at various settings, including Bannerman Island, where she had met Angelika.

Portale drew her attention to April 29, 2015. She told the court that she had arrived on the island that morning at 9:15.

"Did you have an occasion to go back to Cornwall Yacht Club again?"

"I did," Susan said. "Someone called and said Angelika was coming and I didn't want her to ride alone, so I popped back on the crew boat with the captain and went back to the yacht club."

"Who did you travel back to the Cornwall Yacht Club with?"

"Just the captain. When we got off, Miss Graswald and a friend of hers were arriving."

"Okay. What happened next?"

"Well, I greeted her and said that I was sorry and she introduced me to her friend."

"And can you describe what was Miss Graswald doing, anything at that time that you observed?"

"She was nervous."

"Was she making anything?"

"She had brought some supplies to make a wreath to honor her fiancé."

"Were you present at the Cornwall Yacht Club at that time when Miss Graswald had made a phone call to the police?" Portale asked.

"Yes."

"And did you hear that phone call . . . ?"

"Yes, she had it on speaker."

"And what happened?"

"She called them and said, 'Are you coming to—are you coming to . . .'" Susan paused. "I want to make sure I'm saying it right, the way she said it. 'Are you coming to my ceremony for Vinny?' And the response was, 'We're going to try to get there. We're going to try to get there.' And that was pretty much the conversation."

She then traveled back to the island with the captain, Angelika, and her friend Katie at about 12:30.

"So, as you arrived on Bannerman's Island, did you observe anyone on the dock?" Portale asked.

"As we arrived, yes. The detectives were all there and their boats."

"When you say 'detectives,' you mean the New York State Police?"

"I would assume that's what they were, yes."

"When Miss Graswald arrived on the dock, did she speak to any civilians?"

"I don't think there were any. I don't remember there being any civilians on the dock. All the civilians that I know, I'll call them volunteers, they were working. They were up on the island."

"By the way, is Bannerman's Island a public island?"

"No. . . . I don't live in New York. I think it's a state park now. It used to be privately owned. You cannot go without a tour. It's not open to the public."

"So, it's fair to say that anyone who would have been on Bannerman's Island that day would have been a volunteer?" Portale clarified.

"Absolutely."

". . . How were the New York State Police dressed?"

"Business casual. Nicely dressed," she said, contradicting the investigators' testimony that two of the three had worn jeans and T-shirts.

"And did you observe Miss Graswald disembark from the boat?"

"Yes."

"Was she smoking a cigarette?"

"Yes, she was."

"And what happened?"

"They told her to put it out, [that] they've been waiting a long time for us." This definitely didn't coincide with the investigators' description of a warm welcome.

"What happened next?"

"We got off the boat and Miss Graswald tried to introduce us to the crew of people, and they didn't seem to be interested in me. And they went up, it's a staircase, they followed her up the stairs."

"What was Miss Graswald's demeanor at that point?"

"She knew them and she was going to show them the island."

"Do you recall whether she was carrying a flotation, flowers, for Mr. Viafore?"

"Was she carrying it? I don't remember," Susan said. "I know we brought it on the boat. I don't remember who took it off the boat. It could have been her friend or it could have been, I think—I was a little overwhelmed at seeing this group of police or detectives, whatever they were, and I don't remember who took it off. I do know it came with us to the island."

"Do you know any of the police investigators by name?" Portale asked.

"The only one I know by name is his last name, De-Quarto."

"And can you describe any of the others?"

"That were there? The guy that seemed to be in charge was six feet tall, medium to a little heavy build, dark hair, Italian looking."

"And did there come a time when you came to observe Miss Graswald sitting on the trail?"

"Yes," Susan said. "I was there a while and I was walking around, and I heard them speaking so I came down to see what they were doing. And she was there and she was crying and the three men were around her and questioning her and interrogating her."

Julie Mohl objected to the characterization and the judge ordered that the word "interrogating" be stricken from the record. Portale asked her to describe what she'd observed without using that word.

"They were bullying her, she was crying," Susan said.

Mohl objected again on the same grounds, but this time she was overruled.

Asked to continue, Susan explained, "It was obvious to anyone that it was not a good situation. She was unhappy and crying. I didn't want her to be alone and I said, 'Do you want me to stay with you?'"

"And what happened at that point, if anything?"

"She said, 'No, it's okay,' and the police or detectives said, 'She really doesn't need you, it's okay.'"

"Who said that?" Portale asked.

"I don't want to guess, but I think it was the big guy. I don't know his name, sorry."

"You said that you could hear what was going on . . . do you remember what the questions were about?"

"'Why were you here at the building?' Her response was [that] she was cold, it was getting cold. 'Why were you taking pictures of that,' 'why were you'—again, again, repetitive, repetitive."

"So, at some point did you then leave?"

"Well, I looked at her and she said, 'It's okay,'" Susan said. "They told me it was okay and so I said, 'Well, I'm here if you need me.' I walked away, and you can't go very far. I went back to work. I was just weeding."

"And about how far away did you go?"

"I'm not very good at distances," she told the attorney, with an apologetic grimace.

"Just do your best," Portale assured her.

"A hundred yards. Four hundred yards. Well, a football field is a hundred yards?"

"Yes."

"I was around the corner, down not very far."

"Did you continue to hear what was going on?"

"No. I walked away."

"Did there come a time when you approached again?"

"I came back," Susan said. "I wanted to see what was going on and I heard more voices as I approached. They were still, she was still crying. It was a little more agitated and I said, 'Do you want me to stay? Really, I think I should be here with you.' And she, again, quietly said, 'No, it's okay,' and they said, 'She's okay.' And I just looked at her and said, 'Are you okay?' and she said, 'I'm fine.' And so, I think she didn't want to involve me."

ADA Mohl objected one more time and was sustained. Portale moved on without argument. "So, how many times total did you approach them as they sat on the trail?"

"Three."

"Did there come a time when Miss Graswald left the island?"

"Yes."

"About how long after you last approached the group did she leave the island?"

"Half an hour," Susan estimated.

"Did there come a time later when you spoke to the police?"

"Yes, at the police barracks. I followed the police."

After another squabble between opposing counsel, the judge sustained the state's objection. Portale turned the witness over to prosecutor Julie Mohl.

CHAPTER THIRTY-ONE

Julie Mohl walked Susan McCardell back through her direct testimony and then got down to more serious questioning. "Prior to getting back on the boat to Bannerman's Island with the defendant, did you hear a phone call between the defendant and a member of the police?"

"Yes."

"After that phone call, you didn't hear Miss Graswald say, 'I don't want to go out to Bannerman's anymore,' did you?"

"Forever?" Susan asked.

"No, that day. She didn't say to you, 'Susan I don't want to go over there anymore,' did she?"

"No."

"And when she arrived to Bannerman's Island, she didn't seem surprised that the police were there?"

"She called them," Susan pointed out.

"Right. So she knew they were going to be there, correct?"

"She called and asked them to go, yes. They said they would try to get there. So, she was happy to see them," she said, contradicting her own testimony of the investigators' surly statement about Angelika's cigarette.

Portale objected. "She doesn't know whether Miss Graswald was surprised. She can testify to observations, but she doesn't know whether or not my client—"

The judge cut him off with one word: "Sustained."

"She asked them to go to the island; is that right, ma'am?" Mohl asked.

Portale objected. "Asked and answered."

"Overruled; you can answer," the judge intoned.

"Yes, she asked them—she was going to do a ceremony for Vinny—'Are you guys gonna come?' and they said they would try to get there."

"And her demeanor was happy; is that right?"

"Yes."

"In fact, she greeted one of them with a hug; is that right?"

"I don't remember that."

"And she introduced you to them?"

"Yes."

"And you stated that they went up the stairs and off on the trail . . . at that time, you did not go with them; is that fair to say?"

"I went shortly thereafter."

"And where did you go?"

"I was with Katie and we just took a walk and I showed her the different sides of the island she had never been on."

"So, you gave her a tour of the island?"

"Yes."

"And then you stated you came over to check on Angelika?"

"Yes."

"And when you came over to check on her, she stated she was okay and you asked if she needed anything and she said no, correct?"

"I asked her, I said, 'Are you okay?,' and she looked, obviously not okay."

"Objection, Your Honor, not responsive," the ADA said.

The defense took umbrage at that. "She didn't give the answer she wants and now she wants to strike it."

"It was not responsive to the question," Mohl said.

"Actually, it is responsive," Portale argued.

"I'll decide that," the judge said, "And I think it is. The answer stays. Continue."

"Can she finish with her answer?" Mohl asked.

"I'm not sure—" the judge began.

Susan spoke up. "I'm finished. I mean, it was obvious to me and I think it was obvious to anyone she should not be alone with these three men talking to her like that so—"

Judge Freehill stopped her. "That's something of a different answer."

"Well, not really," Susan said.

"Continue, Ms. Mohl," the judge told the attorney

"She stated to you that she was okay?"

"She did."

"And you came over a second time and, again, she stated she was okay?"

"She did."

"And you stated you went over there a third time. . . . And again, she stated she was okay?"

"She told me she was okay."

"After each time you left, you never sent over a different volunteer to check on her, did you?"

"No."

"And you never heard as you were walking away, 'Wait, Susan, help me, help me,' did you?" Mohl asked.

"No."

Prosecutor Mohl took Susan through a series of questions about any conversations she'd had with the defense attorney or any investigator on the defense team. Susan insisted that the first conversation had been the evening before.

"Ms. McCardell, you've known Miss Graswald for over a year; is that right?"

"That's right."

"And in fact, you stated in a prior conversation with investigators that, of all people that you have volunteered with at Bannerman's, you're the closest to her; is that right?"

Susan agreed.

"And in fact, you've gone to visit her at the Orange County Jail, haven't you?"

"That is correct."

Mohl then tried to argue that the defense was not in compliance with the Rosario rule, a commonly used statute in New York criminal cases. According to the Rosario rule, the prosecution is required to turn over to the defense any reports regarding the anticipated testimony of the witnesses they call. The defense is required to do the same, with one exception—they do not need to provide anything regarding the defendant if their client intends to take the stand. The defense, however, had not provided the prosecution with a report regarding Susan's expected testimony.

Portale responded in a self-righteous tone and then pointed the finger at the prosecution, insisting they turn over any reports on his witness to the defense.

His words provoked a testy response from the judge: "Why would you say that as if I didn't know that?"

"I was trying to remind you, Your Honor," Portale answered, digging a deeper hole.

"You don't need to remind me," the judge bit back.

When Julie Mohl passed on the witness, the judge spoke to Susan directly. "Out of this approximately ten volunteers, this crew, was there a person that was in charge?"

"Well, we have a person in charge of the gardeners and then we have—"

"On-site?"

"On-site. We're volunteers, or adult volunteers in charge of gardening. And then there's people that, yes, she was there, she is in charge, yes."

"And . . . what was her name?"

"Her name is . . ." Susan hesitated. "I'm sorry, I'm nervous."

"Don't be nervous," the judge urged.

"I can't even believe I'm blanking on it."

"It's not that important."

"I can give it to you. . . . Donna is her name."

"So when your group of volunteers arrived en masse, did Donna parcel you out where you should go, or was this a routine that you knew where you should go?"

"It was the first time of the season," Susan explained. "So, it's a little broadsided to be on the island because you can't go the rest of the year. There's a little more looking around than usual and checking around from the season and she assigns—"

"So, everyone has their own particular spots?"

"They have comfort zones, they have gardens they call their own."

"How many acres?" the judge asked.

"I think it's like four. It could be seven. It's built like a volcano."

"The area you observed the BCI investigators speaking to the defendant, was that one of her comfort zones?"

"I wouldn't think so, it's on the trail."

The judge asked Portale if he had any redirect and the attorney asked Susan to explain their brief conversation before court that morning. She testified that he had simply directed her to the third floor.

Mohl was invited to recross and she, too, was brief. "Ma'am, had you seen Miss Graswald on the trail before?"

"You have to use it to get anywhere," Susan confirmed. With that, Susan was released from the witness stand.

With no more witnesses to call, Richard Portale again argued against the use of the interrogation tape at trial. He alleged that Graswald may have miscarried a baby while in police custody, making her more vulnerable and increasing the probability that she could be coerced. An odd assertion, considering he'd previously alleged she was on her period at the time—normally, menstruation does not coincide with pregnancy. In addition, he brought up his client asking, 'Who is Miranda?' after she was read her Miranda Rights. Portale argued that her question demonstrated that she did not grasp the implications of her eleven-hour interview. Investigator Donald De-Quarto, however, had insisted that Angelika understood her rights completely when he'd read them to her and she'd read them to herself.

The two sides bickered over reports, photographs, and the need to keep the hearing open for another day. When ADA Mohl asserted that the defense had rested their case, Portale denied that he had.

"You said you rested, Mr. Portale," Mohl insisted.

"I said I have no further witnesses," Portale argued.

The judge intervened. "We consider that to rest. In Orange County, we use different words for things apparently."

"I never said the words 'I rest,'" Portale maintained. "I said, 'I don't have any more witnesses.' We may recall the same witnesses if—"

"We're not recalling anybody," the judge said. "You're both going to have two weeks to submit memorandums. You have two weeks. Beyond that, you'll be back here for decision."

Chartier chimed in to argue again that the hearing should remain open, but the judge rebuffed his request.

The judge now had to determine if testimony of the unrecorded statements, as well as the video of Angelika's interrogation, could be presented to a jury. Courtroom observers wondered if it was possible for the state to present a case if all of her statements were prohibited from being shown in the courtroom. Prosecutors had little other evidence that pointed directly to guilt.

In five days, seven witnesses had provided information to the court. The judge requested that the state provide him with an English translation of the conversation Angelika had had with the Russian interpreter toward the end of the eleven-hour interview.

The attorneys would have to wait much longer than they'd expected for Judge Freehill to reach his decision.

CHAPTER THIRTY-TWO

In August 2016, Vince's friends and family gathered in the Quiet Cove Riverfront Park to enjoy a barbecue and remember Vince's birthday. The serene location, just north of the Marist College campus, provided stunning views of the length of the Hudson River that Vince had loved so much. They had all come together last August on this spot, but this year there was a new addition—a park bench dedicated to Vince. His friends had set up a GoFundMe page in October 2015 and installed the fixture in April of 2016. It faced the water, and on the four slats of its back was inscribed: "Gone but never forgotten, Always in our hearts, Vinny Viafore, Till We Meet Again."

Laura Rice told the *Poughkeepsie Journal* that her brother "had more friends than anybody I know. His friends were family, too. They keep his memory alive. They loved him. You don't have those kind of friends if you're not a good person."

The original date for the judge to deliver his decision on the evidence presented during the Huntley Hearing was

July 28, 2016. But that day passed without a decision, and the months slipped to September and then to December. Finally, on the sixteenth of that month, the two parties gathered once more before the bench.

Judge Freehill ruled that the state could not present evidence regarding the contradictory statements Angelika had made to Officer Bedetti about the whereabouts of her cell phone, nor could they submit anything Angelika had said in the car when she rode from the Newburgh waterfront to the state police barracks on April 29.

As for the eleven-hour interrogation video, the judge ruled that the majority of it was admissible. However, he blocked the portion of the conversation with a Russian interpreter "because a finding . . . [could not] be made that the statements were voluntary."

Relief wafted from the prosecution table like a sigh. Had the ruling gone the other way, trying Angelika for second-degree murder would have been a quixotic quest. Without the defendant's own damning words, the chance of a guilty verdict was slim to infinitesimal.

The defense was disappointed by the decision, but Portale still had another maneuver in his back pocket, ready to play when the time was right.

The judge wrapped up by scheduling jury selection for the trial to begin on February 14, 2017, as well as another pretrial hearing on January 23.

In due course, jury selection was moved to March. But days before the new date, the defense threw another obstacle into the timetable by filing a notice of intent to present psychiatric evidence, based on an examination of Angelika in July 2015. Forensic psychologist Marc Janoson, who conducted the analysis, had more than thirty years of experience in the field of psychological assessment and had testified frequently in the courtroom.

Angelika's legal team alleged that the police had

coerced a confession during her long interview at the barracks. They argued that Janoson would testify at trial that Angelika had "exhibited traits—such as higher levels of suggestibility—that would render her vulnerable to producing a false confession." In the psychologist's report, filed in court, he assessed that Angelika was afflicted with "paranoid mania" and possessed "many of the known psychological characteristics of persons who make false confessions." Janoson found Angelika to be "manic, inflated and grandiose, impulsive and lacking in judgement." He wrote: "This lack of judgement and tendency to run off at the mouth is likely what happened during her interrogation. Her overactive, energetic, and self-dramatizing behaviors may explain why she posted a photo doing a cartwheel after her fiancé's death."

Using her responses to a psychometric testing tool, he believed she "had learned to numb herself emotionally after having had traumatic experiences with other people" and that she was "rated as not being sadistic, cruel, vindictive, predatory, controlling/dominating, or particularly aggressive."

Prosecutor David Byrne objected strongly, citing law requiring that the defense give notice of intent within thirty days of their not guilty plea. He argued that Portale "never gave the people the required notice. He chose to keep us in the dark . . . I don't see any good cause." Byrne went on to ask the judge to consider imposing sanctions on the defense team.

In their legal filing to fight against the use of Janoson's testimony, ADA John Geidel wrote: "When an extremely late notice is filed, the principles of fairness and time efficiency have been eradicated." The prosecution went on to argue that, because they had not been able to evaluate Angelika in the same time frame, any analysis performed now would be "rendered useless."

Part of the prosecution's countermeasure to stop the defense's psychiatric testimony was a report from their own forensic psychiatrist, Sandra Antoniak, from May 2016. She'd reviewed Angelika's medical records, her jail violations records, and other documents to reach her conclusions. She believed that Angelika was mentally normal at the time she was arrested but had been determined to be a suicide risk because the extreme nature of her recent experiences and her reaction to them.

Antoniak alleged that the length of time between Angelika's evaluation by Janoson and the submission of the filing "would render it impossible for the people's expert to reach a meaningful conclusion regarding false confession." In other words, the state could not accurately assess if Angelika was faking a mental illness or not. After two years of incarceration, Angelika's memory would have faded and her state of mind would not be the same.

Portale, however, claimed that he did indeed have good cause to file when he had. It came about, the defense attorney claimed, because the prosecution had "poached" an expert the defense planned to use and "intentionally" withheld evidence, referring to the videotape of the interrogation in which the audio had been enhanced.

The defense insisted that if the testimony was left out their client would be deprived due process of law, making any trial verdict defective and subject to an overturning on appeal. Judge Freehill ruled that the "conscious decision to withhold the report of the forensic psychologist [was] not justified." Nonetheless, he allowed Angelika's attorneys to proceed with a false confession defense and file notice of psychiatric evidence. He added that "the people will be given the opportunity to examine Miss Graswald, as is their right." With that, the judge announced a trial date of June 13 and warned the attorneys to stick to it. "We're going to be bringing in a great influx of jurors, so this date . . . it's very important to keep it."

Wrapping up court matters, the defense said that they had given the state all of the material from the forensic psychologist, except for the final report, which they had not yet received. The prosecution requested a HIPAA (Health Insurance Portability and Accountability Act) waiver for Graswald in order to access her previous psychiatric history. They also renewed their request to subpoena ABC News and News 12 for broadcast tapes and unaired footage of interviews with Angelika—before and after her arrest—to aid in their psychiatric evaluation.

In May, the defense confirmed that they intended to prove at trial that Angelika had falsely confessed to killing her fiancé. The prosecution's psychological expert was scheduled to deliver a report by the end of July. The June date of the trial was pushed to August 15. At times, it was difficult for the family to believe that it would ever come to an end.

On July 17, 2017, the parties met in court. It appeared as if the trial was on track to begin the next month. According to defense attorney Richard Portale, prosecutors had approached him that week with an offer to drop the charges against his client to manslaughter. He said, however, that he turned it down, because he wouldn't accept a deal unless it allowed Angelika to be released before the end of the year.

But on Monday, July 24, everything changed.

Deputies escorted Angelika into the courtroom, wearing an orange jumpsuit with a long-sleeved T-shirt underneath. Her long ponytail hung down over the shoulder onto the front of her body.

The district attorney's office announced that, after extensive consultation with Vince's family, they had reached a plea bargain deal with the defendant. The revised charge:

criminally negligent homicide. This meant that the defendant did not intentionally cause the victim's death, but the accused's actions or inactions had created a risk that was not justifiable.

Prior to this agreement, Angelika had faced second-degree murder and manslaughter charges, which would have resulted in a sentence of fifteen years to life in prison. The sentence she faced with the new charge was short—fifteen months to four years.

For nearly two years, Angelika had proclaimed her absolute innocence, but with this deal she was now willing to acknowledge some degree of responsibility in Vince's death.

The judge asked for her plea.

"Guilty," she said.

"You are pleading guilty voluntarily?" Freehill confirmed.

"Yes, Your Honor," Angelika answered.

He then asked if she understood that by accepting this agreement she was agreeing to abandon her right to "appeal both the conviction and the ultimate sentence to a higher court for review." That meant, he said, that she was waiving her "right to appeal and that after you plead and are sentenced, no further review of the plea and sentence will occur, and the plea and sentence will be final and irrevocable."

Angelika agreed.

She admitted to criminal negligence by removing a drain plug from Vince's kayak, knowing that the weather was dangerous and being aware of the size of the waves. She also acknowledged that she'd known the water temperature was forty degrees and that the locking clip on one of his paddles was missing. She agreed that she'd known Vince was not wearing a life jacket or a wet suit. She acknowledged that all those things created a risk of death and that she had failed to perceive it. By the end of her admissions, she was sobbing, her hands covering her nose and mouth.

The judge asked, "His kayak took on water and began to sink, correct?"

"Yes," she said. She stared hard at the floor by her feet.

He set her sentencing for November 1, 2017. In October, that date was delayed by a week.

On the way out of the courtroom, Mary Ann Viafore did not stand still for an interview. In passing, she told the press, "I miss my son—that's what's running through my heart." Across the country, every mother's heart clenched in response to her pain.

CHAPTER THIRTY-THREE

The *New York Post* made their feelings about the plea deal clear in a headline that read: "A Light Paddling After Guilty Plea." Many who remembered Vince in the Poughkeepsie area agreed, feeling betrayed by the legal system.

The day after Angelika's guilty plea, Orange County District Attorney David Hoovler called a news conference in an attempt to justify the agreement and point to the silver lining in the cloud of justice. "Yesterday, as you are aware, . . . [Angelika] pled guilty to criminally negligent homicide on the agreement that she would be sentenced to the maximum prison sentence for the charge of one and one-third years to four years in state prison.

"There is little direct precedent, if any, in New York, for a homicide conviction for removing a plug in a kayak. The kayak used was not designed for river use, such as in the Hudson River, and was considered an inferior model. The victim was also likely aware of the water conditions, the temperature; he knew he was not wearing a life jacket or a wet suit—facts that the jury might use in weighing the victim's state of mind in the matter. Also, alcohol was present.

"The district attorney's office purchased a kayak identical to the one the victim had and conducted experiments with the state police and experts—may I add—extensive experiments, leading us to conclude [that] in rough water, the kayak would fill with water if the plug was removed and the occupant was the same height and weight as the victim. When the kayak was filled with water, its performance specifications would be diminished. Notwithstanding those experiments, during the course of the investigation, a picture that predates the homicide was found with the victim in the water without having a plug in it."

Hoovler went on to discuss the late submission of the psychiatric evidence implying a false confession. He said that the year and a half that had lapsed since Angelika's arrest had given her sufficient time to prepare for an examination with a state-appointed mental health expert, rendering any new determination useless.

Richard Portale also expressed his ambivalence. He said he'd had to consider the potential of a long sentence for his client if the case moved to trial. "We knew we had a good case and we knew they had a good case in a lot of ways. As worried as Hoovler was about an acquittal, Ms. Graswald's side was worried about a conviction. When you have situations where both sides are a little bit uncomfortable, that's when deals get done."

Plea bargain agreements seldom satisfy either side, and this case was no exception, judging by the public statements of both parties involved. However, it was not difficult to assume that the defense team was in a celebratory mood.

Aside from the actual sentencing, one big question

remained. Would Angelika Graswald get the insurance money after she admitted to some blame in Vince's death? It was a legal conundrum. State legal precedent, known as the "slayer rule," prevented killers in New York State from profiting off reprehensible conduct that contributed to another person's death. However, this had never been codified into law. Slayer rule decisions were made based on prior court decisions. Most experts felt that she probably wouldn't receive the money, but there was doubt because of the nature of her charge.

For the moment, Richard Portale put that question to rest. He announced that his client didn't "have any plans to try to fight for the money. I'm sure of that."

CHAPTER THIRTY-FOUR

On September 26, 2017, a Poughkeepsie-based non-profit called Family Services sponsored the National Day of Remembrance for Murder Victims down by the waterfront. Congress had established this special day in 2007 to honor homicide victims and provide comfort for the impact of long-term trauma on families and communities.

A roll call of those who had been killed in Dutchess County was read to the hushed crowd: Katie Filberti, a teenager sexually assaulted and murdered in 2011; Patricia and Shawn Wonderley, who died when a suspect evading arrest by City of Poughkeepsie Police broadsided their van in 2012; and, of course, Vincent Viafore, who drowned in the Hudson River in 2015.

On October 27, 2017, Vince's family filed a wrongful death lawsuit against Angelika in the State Supreme Court, Dutchess County. In the documents, they claimed that Angelika's negligence, recklessness, and carelessness made her responsible for the death of their loved one. The damages they sought were unspecified.

Unlike the criminal case against her, this civil case required less proof to get a favorable decision. Rather than the "beyond reasonable doubt" standard, the plaintiffs only had to prove that a preponderance of evidence existed—more supporting their side than the other—to have Angelika declared civilly liable.

Laws vary from state to state, but in New York plaintiffs are limited to seeking reparation for the potential economic loss caused by the death—how many years the victim would have been anticipated to work and his or her potential pay during that period of time. In addition, pain and suffering can only be assessed if the victim can be shown to have experienced one or the other, or both. No value is placed on the grief of his loved ones. Occasionally, punitive damages can be added if the defendant's misconduct involves reckless regard or malice.

For the Viafore family, as for many other victims' families, the money is not the point. They seek accountability for Vince's death and the Viafores wanted to limit Angelika's ability to make money off of it.

On November 5, Richard Portale filed an appeal on Angelika's behalf. Since her agreement to waive the right to appeal when she'd pleaded guilty contained wording that she could not appeal after her sentencing, Portale turned in the paperwork three days prior to her sentencing day on November 8.

On that day, Angelika entered the courtroom to listen to the most painful part of all the court proceedings: the victim impact statements.

Vince's childhood friend Kevin Beisswinger's speech was indicative of the feelings of many of Vince's lifelong acquaintances.

"Vin was one of a kind, and he is greatly missed. When I heard the news that my friend, Vin Viafore, was missing on April 19, 2015, I was devastated and heartbroken, not just for me, but for so many people that I knew Vin had touched over the years. To know Vin was to love Vin. Once you were a friend of Vin's, you had a friend for life. So many who were lucky enough to call him a friend know exactly what I mean when I say that.

"Angelika, of course, we now know, was involved. She took the life of a dear friend, son, brother, uncle. She, the person he had loved through ups and downs, had betrayed him. I wake up at night sometimes, shaking, thinking about how he must have felt in his final moments, betrayed by the woman he loved. There is no sentence available for this crime that she has pled to that is sufficient in my eyes.

"Vin was the center that kept so many of us connected over the years. He was always organizing get-togethers when someone who had moved away was home visiting. He was a trusted friend whom I could lean on for advice and could count on for a compassionate ear. He was taken from all of us, and the world is simply less without Vin in it. I am especially heartbroken for Vin's family, his wonderful mother, Mary Ann, his sister Laura, his ex-wife Sue, who he loved to the end. They, we, all deserve justice. They all deserve better. Vin deserved so much better."

The next heart-stopping statement came from Vince's sister, Laura Rice.

"On April 19, 2015, my brother Vinny died a very tragic death, and the lives of all who loved him will never be the same. When I think of my brother's last moments alive, I think of the pain he must have endured and I visualize him trying to survive hypothermia in the freezing-cold river, confused and not understanding why the woman who said she loved him and wanted to marry him did nothing to help him.

"Over the past two and a half years, my family and I have quietly sat back through multiple adjournments, inaccurate statements, and accusations against my brother, so I would like to take this opportunity to tell you about Vinny and the wonderful person that Angelika took away from us all.

"Vinny was my little brother, always wanted to be included and following me around like my shadow. He grew up fast, and from the little boy his family called 'little Vinny' he became an amazing person. He was loyal, dedicated, brave, and fearless—living every day to the fullest.

"Vinny was a caring person. When he would see someone in need, he wouldn't think twice about helping them. He would stop and give a homeless person a few dollars. And when the little girl next door had a problem with her bike tire my brother, as usual, delayed what he was doing and took her to the bike shop to get her tire fixed.

"He touched many lives and gave so much to the people around him. . . .

"Vinny was a special person with a huge heart and was loved by so many people. After eighteen years of marriage, he had a special relationship with his former wife Sue. He had more friends than anyone I have ever known, and these friends are truly amazing people. In fact, during the time he was missing, they never gave up on the search for him or the support of our family. Since this tragedy occurred, they have shown their love with their ongoing messages, tributes to his life, and annual gatherings respecting his life and legacy.

"My brother and I were very close. We talked often and were always there for each other. One of the hardest things for me, as a parent, is seeing how his death impacted my children. Vinny was very close to them and for my son, Michael, Vinny was the big brother, always including him and spending time with him. My son will forever be affected by the loss of his uncle. As for my daughter,

Melissa, Vinny was the fun uncle and made her feel special. She now has a daughter and it is especially hard knowing that she will never get to meet her great-uncle, who would have adored his grandniece.

"As for my mother, there are no words that can describe how she feels losing a child, especially her only son. This truly is one of the most devastating events a mother can go through, especially when the death is so tragic and caused intentionally by someone else. Her life will never be the same.

"My brother did not deserve to have his life end this way. Our family feels Angelika should be held accountable for the actions she admitted to, where a short four-year sentence does not seem just. Furthermore, serving a portion of that sentence seems even more unjust. Also, we strongly believe that this injustice is brutally difficult to deal with and, in turn, Angelika, as a non-citizen of the USA, should be immediately deported upon completing her sentence.

". . . Vinny is missed every day and will never be forgotten while he remains in our hearts forever."

Speaking to the judge, ADA David Byrne said, "The defendant through her criminally negligent actions left the world a lesser place. Vincent Viafore was beloved. He was a good person, he was a decent person. He was a true friend."

Richard Portale made no comments during the sentencing session. Judge Freehill asked Graswald if she wanted to speak.

"No, thank you," she said.

In his sentencing, Freehill dug in with sharp comments about Angelika. "It is apparent that you have some kind of narcissistic personality disorder. Was it removing a plug from the kayak, which appears to have been done months ago? Was it tampering with the clip on his paddle? Not really. It was the immediate acts of you being in your kayak and Vincent floundering in the water and you not taking any steps to try to help him and your failure to perceive a substantial risk."

Referencing the comments Angelika had made to police, the judge said that they demonstrated that "you certainly have a lack of understanding of other people's feelings. It appears to me you have an excessive need for admiration. You exhibit such exaggerated feelings of self-worth and Vincent Viafore was the unnecessary victim of that."

Mentioning her two previous divorces, he said that she understood how to end "unsatisfactory relationships in a manner that would be socially and legally acceptable. You could have walked out on Vinny if you were unhappy, rather than whatever it was in your mind that led to removing the plug and the other acts you took."

With that, he pronounced the sentence: one and a third to four years in state prison, as agreed. With time served, only forty-two days remained in her mandated incarceration. The judge added a five-thousand-dollar fine, to which the defense objected, since it hadn't been mentioned in the plea deal.

Outside of the courthouse, Richard Portale read a statement that Angelika had prepared: "'Never would I have imagined waking up one day and finding myself behind bars, charged with murdering the man I love.

"'The entire process has been incredibly difficult for me. I love Vince very much and miss him terribly. When we went kayaking that day, my intention was for both of us to come home. But, [from] the moment I was pulled from the water—they labeled me a defendant. I don't believe I was treated fairly. This entire process has been incredibly one-sided and unjust. I've learned so much about the system. I've learned that you are not innocent until proven guilty. I foolishly placed my trust in people who didn't deserve it and it cost me dearly.

"'I am not a murderer. I've said that from the beginning. If I could do anything to bring Vince back, I would.

"'I'd like to extend my deepest gratitude to my friends, family, and legal team who believed in me and fought against all odds for my release. And to those who haven't even met me yet [who] showed me so much love and support.

"'I have now been in jail for over two years. Once I am released, I will try and put my life back together again. I'm hoping to see my sister Jelena, who had a baby while I was in jail, and to hug my mom and dad again, and mourn the loss of my grandmother who died while I was behind bars.

"'I hope that, with this legal battle behind us, we can all begin to heal. I send my condolences to the Viafore family and to my own family, who have had to walk this hell beside me—although from across the world. May God heal us all.'"

Angelika's only reference to Vince's family was a perfunctory one—stuck at the end like an afterthought. It seemed to prove the judge's point about the self-absorption of the woman who had just been convicted of criminally negligent homicide.

As Mary Viafore emerged from the courthouse after sentencing, Blaise Gomez of News 12 Westchester approached her. "How are you feeling?"

"I believe that justice was not served for my son," she said. "We're not happy with the sentence. It's the law— we couldn't do anything about it—but four years for taking someone's life? No way."

By now, a flock of reporters had surrounded Mary Ann, her daughter, and her lawyer. Another reporter said, "We listened to your daughter, that must have been tough."

"Yes, yes, it was."

"What do you have to say about what she had to say?"

"Well, she was right on the money. My son was a good man and everyone loved him," Mary Ann said, her voice strangled with emotion. "We miss him very much and so, that's all we have to say."

"One last question," another reporter asked, "because she didn't say anything to you. She didn't turn around. Were you expecting it or did that not even matter?"

"No, it didn't," Mary Ann said firmly. "I never want to see her again if I don't have to."

A different reporter spoke up. "Out here, her lawyer read a statement on her behalf saying that she was a victim of the process, that she is not a murderer. And that she expected to come home with Vincent that day they went out kayaking."

As she listened, Mary Ann shook her head in disbelief. "I don't believe a word she said."

Mary Ann's lawyer stepped in. "The closing statement from the judge said it all, and that's how we all feel. And he was just as angry as we were in this case. We believe in the American justice system and we do not believe in the sentencing of it all, but it is over and we need to go on."

CHAPTER THIRTY-FIVE

Under sunny skies, with her hair pulled up in a high ponytail and wearing a gray parka, tan pants, white shirt, and white athletic shoes, Angelika Graswald walked out of the Bedford Hills Correctional Facility for Women on Thursday, December 21, 2017, about six weeks after her sentencing. With Richard Portale by her side carrying a full grocery bag, she walked over to a vehicle and climbed into the back seat. The driver placed the bag in the hatchback compartment, got up front, and drove through the jail gates.

Once off the grounds of the incarceration facility, the vehicle parked. Portale and Angelika got out of the car and approached a wide array of microphones beside a busy street. Two women emerged from the vehicle. One pointed a camera at reporters, recording them as Portale read a statement to the gathered media. Angelika stood quietly by her attorney. As he spoke, she looked at the passing traffic, down at the ground, and up at Portale's face.

Addressing the crowd, Portale said, "Angelika is grateful to be here today. She's grateful for this day. She's excited to be able to reconnect with her family in a meaningful way. She plans to FaceTime with her family as soon as we can. She's grateful to be able to breathe in the fresh air, walk in the fresh air. But, to be sure, reconnecting is going to be difficult, and reconstructing her life is going to be difficult. Her day-to-day, her reality, is much different today than it was thirty-two months ago. She's excited to be able to do that and, at this point, we're going to get started. So, thank you very much. We're not going to take any questions, but I want to say, we appreciate all of you for having covered her story in a fair and evenhanded manner. We do appreciate that. Thank you."

The two returned to the waiting vehicle and drove away from the jail and the press. A man, who identified himself as one of Portale's lawyers, followed in a Range Rover. He hopped from lane to lane, preventing any press vehicles from pursuing the car carrying Angelika. On his erratic journey, he cut off a school bus and stopped at a green light to foil the dogged media.

After losing them all, Angelika and company pulled up to a white-tablecloth surf 'n' turf eatery, the Lexington Square Café in Mount Kisco. Lawyer, client, and the two women went into a private room on the second floor, where their meal began with martinis all around. Angelika ordered a thirty-eight-dollar steak, cooked medium.

When Angelika had pleaded guilty, Richard Portale had initially told the media that she absolutely was not going to attempt to claim Vince's life insurance money. Now his statement was laden with uncertainty. "I can't comment on whether she will [ever] try to collect the claim. This is still ongoing and there are so many variables pending."

After her release, Angelika would have to spend sixteen months on parole living in a halfway house in Orange County. The possibility of deportation hung over her head.

* * *

In January 2018, the amount of the insurance payo[ut]
which would have gone to Angelika if Vince's death ha[d]
been natural or by accident—was revealed to be higher
than previously reported. Instead of a quarter of a million
dollars, she was to receive 45 percent of the policies, for a
total of $545,000.

On January 16, Laura Rice appeared before Judge
James Pagones of the Dutchess County Surrogate Court,
asking that the court confirm that Angelika had forfeited
her rights to any assets when she'd admitted her responsibility for Vince's death. The judge ruled that the court was
required to conduct a hearing and that Vince's family had
a burden to present "a preponderance of credible evidence"
to prove that Angelika's actions on April 19, 2015, were
reckless. The legal definition of one "recklessly" causing
the death of another person required that the perpetrator
was "aware and consciously disregarded a substantial and
unjustifiable risk that such a result . . . [would] occur or
that such circumstance . . . [existed]. The risk must be of
such nature and degree that disregard thereof constitutes
a gross deviation from the standard of conduct that a reasonable person would observe in the situation."

Most of the public believe that if you are found guilty
of causing someone's death you cannot benefit from it.
However, there are limitations. If the court had found
Angelika guilty of first or second-degree murder or manslaughter, the situation would be different. But because
she'd pleaded guilty to criminally negligent homicide, she
was placed in the same category as those who had committed involuntary manslaughter. The court would decide
the outcome.

The family continued to wage a legal battle to prevent
Angelika from getting any proceeds from the insurance
policies. They felt that Portale was doing his best to drag out
the procedures, and those delays were costing them a great

deal of money. They put the civil wrongful death case on hold to await the outcome of the case on the insurance, because legal costs were too expensive to pursue both at the same time.

On January 25, 2018, in Albany, New York, Woodbury Democrat Assemblyman James Skoufis introduced a bill that would cause an automatic forfeiture of life insurance payouts when the beneficiary was determined to be guilty of any involuntary manslaughter charge, including criminally negligent homicide. If this bill was passed, the "slayer rule" that New York judges have followed since a court of appeals decision 130 years ago would finally be codified.

In a press release, Skoufis said, "This isn't simply a matter of finances and insurance, it's a matter of justice. Any life insurance benefit ought to go to a loved one, not a convict who is intrinsically responsible for the person's death. Individuals like Angelika Graswald should never see a penny of insurance money from their homicide victim's policy."

The final chapter of the legal battle was settled in August 2018. It was decided that the Viafore family and Angelika would share the insurance money; the amount of Angelika's portion was not disclosed.

In addition, Angelika dropped the appeal of her conviction, and the Viafore family ended their wrongful death civil suit against her. The Viafores' attorney reported that the family was "happy it was now all behind them."

Whatever the amount, Angelika will not directly benefit from the financial windfall. She signed over any money she would receive from the life insurance policies to her legal team. The cost of her defense exceeded $1 million.

In February 2018, *20/20* aired an updated story on Angelika's case. In Richard Portale's interview with the show, he continued to cast doubt on the state's case.

"When [. . . the police] realized there was a gun miss. that's when they really cranked it up, 'cause that's when they thought that she maybe shot him."

The state police investigators denied that allegation. They'd learned very quickly that the missing weapon was in the possession of Vince's second wife, Suzanne Viafore. Had the investigators not located the gun and they suspected it was a murder weapon, they would have immediately rushed to the island with forensic experts to look for any evidence that a gun had been used there.

On the show, Angelika once again claimed that she loved Vince and did not kill him. She took umbrage at the possibility of being deported: "It's not right. I want to be able to choose whether I want to stay here or go."

When she was reminded that others thought that her light sentence meant she'd gotten away with murder, she insisted that there was no murder.

Was this the truth or magical thinking? The only person who knows for sure is Angelika, and she has nothing to gain by admitting to anything more.

AFTERWORD

I wanted him dead, and now he's gone
and I'm okay with that.
Angelika Lipska Graswald during her interrogation

Everyone has an opinion on Angelika Graswald's actions, and every one of them is different—they run the gamut from one extreme to another. Somewhere between a long, careful plan for premeditated murder to just another tragic accident, the answer lies concealed in the shadow of bias and personal perception.

The truth is somewhere in the middle. The one extreme—an intentional first-degree homicide plot—lacks credibility because there were so many events outside of Angelika's control. Yes, her actions with the kayak plug and the paddle ring were contributing factors, but she could not have manipulated other necessary variables, like the ferocity of the approaching storm or its ability to create sufficiently threatening rough water in the Hudson River.

Still, the euphoria she expressed feeling at his death does indeed point to culpability.

The defense claimed that the words caught on the interrogation tape amounted to a false confession. They insisted that their client was coerced and bullied into saying what police wanted to hear. This can be a credible claim, but it is hard to swallow in this case. From the beginning, Angelika pointed a finger of guilt at Vince, blaming his sexual proclivities, his failure to go through with the marriage in 2014, and his controlling behavior. These words did not fly out of her mouth after hours of questioning. They erupted first on the island and again in the initial phase of the interrogation.

The theory of accidental death doesn't exactly hold up either. Angelika's behavior in the immediate aftermath of the tragedy—her Facebook posts and her conversations with Vince's friends—demonstrate that she was not just a victim who was lucky to survive a horrendous ordeal. I know everyone grieves differently and I realize that even though Angelika was in this country for years, there were cultural differences, but doing cartwheels in the backyard of Vince's family members is not a reasonable expression of sorrow in any culture.

Angelika's delay of twenty minutes in calling 911 was pivotal in Vince's death. Her admission that she deliberately overturned her own kayak when rescuers were nearby pointed to how she was willing to manipulate the perceptions of others to cover up some measure of her guilt.

The fact that she said she removed his paddle from his reach means she was closer to him than she had tried to make it appear. If she was near enough to grab his paddle, she was in a position to offer more aid. I know many of us would do anything to help a person we loved, even at the risk of losing our own lives. Angelika, however, watched Vince struggle and die while staying safe in her kayak.

What is the truth about the death of Vincent Viafore? We are left holding on to the mushy middle, where total culpability and blamelessness comingle to produce this outcome of a guilty plea and a far-too-short sentence.

Angelika blamed Vince's sexual behavior as the cause of her problems. But how much of that was real and how much was created after the fact to justify her behavior? We don't know. A myriad of possibilities exist.

Vince's mother spoke about Angelika's sexual accusations to journalist Nina Schutzman. "It makes you want to scream at her, at the world, and say, 'That's not true.' Vinny was not like that. She's just dragging him through the mud." His sister added, "I don't know about their sex life, and I don't care to know about it. But I don't believe he is the kind of person that she says he was, in that sense."

Was Angelika like many sociopaths, using smear tactics on the victim to justify their own actions? Or was she being honest about their sex life? Even if she was, she could have left him, as she left other men before. A friend of Angelika told me that threesomes are the desire of every male she's ever encountered in the Poughkeepsie area. Did Angelika latch on to this view of the male population and adopt it as an excuse? Did Vince, like many others, have sexual fantasies that he liked to talk about but never really wanted to execute? We will never know.

Many who knew Vince were shocked by what they perceived as a bias in favor of the defense by the national media. One show provided a demonstration by the defense expert to prove the kayak plug could not have contributed to Vince's death, while failing to mention the tests run by the state that showed the opposite. Others felt that interviews in another show were cherry-picked to present a version of the story that did not reflect the truth.

Was the media's coverage slanted? It is difficult to determine, because the evidence is largely circumstantial. One of the first public voices to speak out against the state's case was Jeanine Pirro, host of the television show *Justice with Judge Jeanine*. Defense attorney Richard Portale had worked for her election campaign when she ran for district attorney, and later worked in her office as an assistant district attorney. Portale and a woman who is an editorial producer for the news department of a major network resided at the same house. Did these relationships with the lead defense attorney color their perceptions? In all likelihood, we will never have a definitive answer to that question either.

From my point of view, Angelika is guiltier of wrongdoing than her sentence indicates. To me, it is clear that she had dark homicidal thoughts before April 19, 2015. Otherwise, much of what she said to investigators on the island and in her interview at the barracks would not have been uttered. Her exclamation that she felt "free" after her admissions on Bannerman indicates someone who felt enslaved by the secrets she kept.

As Laura Rice told the *Poughkeepsie Journal*, "I guess I felt that by her taking a plea, people were going to know that she actually had something to do with it. We will never know all the facts of what happened. But what we do know is, she said she was 'free,' she said, 'He's gone and I'm okay with it,' she felt 'euphoric' after he was gone—you don't just say things like that. She confessed to criminally negligent homicide. I just feel that if you're innocent, you don't plead guilty."

In Angelika's interview with police, she spoke about her angels and demons and how she was torn between the two. She spoke of the freedom she felt when she knew Vince would not make it back to shore. These words do not bloom in a grieving heart. These are deeply felt sentiments that had lurked unspoken for some time.

Did she plot to intentionally kill Vince by any particular means? I doubt it. I think she fantasized about his death and, when the right situation presented itself, she took advantage of it. She acted like an opportunist—ever on the lookout for a chance to make her dark dreams come true.

She moved the paddle out of his reach. She hesitated to call 911 until it was probably too late to save Vince. She faked the capsizing of her own kayak when she knew rescue was imminent.

If there was no plea deal, would Angelika have been found guilty of second-degree murder or manslaughter? I believe there was a strong possibility of conviction. Juries, however, are unpredictable. You only need to look at the Casey Anthony case that I wrote about in *Mommy's Little Girl* to witness that fact. To go to trial posed the risk that Angelika, too, would walk out of the courtroom with no conviction. That outcome would eliminate the only barrier to her claims on Vince's insurance policies. She would have been entitled to her complete share, instead of the portion she received.

The short sentence given to Angelika was painful for those who loved Vince, but an acquittal would have been even worse.

Still, sixteen months for Vince's life feels painfully inadequate. As Michael Goodwin of the *New York Post* put it: "Justice is supposed to be blind, not stupid."

Vincent Alexander Viafore was an ordinary guy with an extraordinary heart who loved life and the people in it and was loved in turn by his family and a legion of friends. His death left a dark, icy void in many who knew him. Rest in Peace, Vinny.

ACKNOWLEDGMENTS

My deepest appreciation goes out to Mary Ann Viafore. She was gracious with her time and with her heart. Talking with her about her son provided me with valuable information and with a sense that, on a basic level, I knew Vinny as a person. I send her my fervent wishes for healing. As a mother, I can only imagine the tremendous pain of her loss.

Thanks to Sean Von Clauss, Stacey Speirs Deneve, Amanda Bopp, and Kimberly Phillips for sharing the memories of Vince. And also to Mike Colvin, Joel Goss, and Sorluna de Butterfly for imparting their recollections of Angelika.

I also appreciate the hard work of Senior Investigator Aniello Moscato, Investigator Donald DeQuarto, and three court reporters: Yvonda Fantroy, Michael DeCelestino, and Cathy Morales.

For invaluable research assistance, I bow deeply to Mary Elizabeth Ciambotti. I am in your debt.

Thanks to Charlie Spicer, Executive Editor at St. Martin's Press, for sticking with me when it went awry, and to

Sarah Grill, who helped me beat this manuscript into submission.

Finally, to my incredible agent of eighteen years, Jane Dystel of Dystel, Goderich & Bourret—without her support, I would not have my long list of published books. And to my wonderful cheerleaders, writer friend Betsy Ashton and Wayne Fanning, the one man capable of keeping me balanced when the sky is falling.